SPAT-OUT

When Profits Over People Affects You

MJ Carver

ISBN: 979-8-9954245-0-5

Imprint: MJ Squared Group

First Edition. Printed in the United States of America.

For permissions or inquiries, contact: mjmj2222@gmail.com

For those who are just starting to build.

The foundation you lay today is the ground you stand on tomorrow.

Contents

Introduction: Before We Begin

This book was not supposed to exist.

I was not planning to write it. I was not sitting at a desk with a blank document and a plan. I was sitting with the particular kind of quiet that follows a layoff — the silence where a calendar full of flights and meetings used to be — and I started writing because I needed to say something I could not find anywhere else.

Not the polished version. Not the LinkedIn post about "exciting new chapter." Not the career advice that pretends a layoff is just a new job opportunity waiting to be reframed.

The real version.

What it actually feels like when a company you gave five years to — sixty percent of your life on the road, your body aging in airport terminals and hotel rooms — decides in a ten-minute meeting that you are a cost worth cutting.

What the system that produced that meeting was actually designed to do.

And what to build on the other side of it so that no system, no quarterly projection, no stranger in an HR meeting can ever put you in that position again.

— — —

This book is for you if you have been laid off, downsized, restructured, or eliminated. If the language your company used was careful and the outcome was blunt. If you showed up, delivered, traveled, sacrificed — and discovered that none of it was a guarantee.

It is for you if you are in the first week or month of shock, still processing what happened. It is for you if you are months out and the initial adrenaline of job searching has given way to something quieter and harder. It is for you if you are employed right now but feeling the instability beneath the surface — the hum of uncertainty that tells you the ground is not as solid as the paycheck suggests.

It is especially for you if you are over forty. If the math of rebuilding feels different at this stage of life than the books written for twenty-five-year-olds suggest it should. If you are looking at the runway ahead and doing the calculation and wondering whether what you have built is enough and whether what you can still build is realistic.

I am in my fifties. I wrote this from inside the experience, not looking back at it from a comfortable distance. The financial stress in these pages is real. The anger is real. The clarity that came from having to look at the system honestly — perhaps for the first time — is real.

— — —

Here is how the book works.

Part One starts where you are right now — in the hit. What it feels like, what it does to your identity and your ego, and why the shame that almost everyone feels is both understandable and misdirected.

Part Two steps back and looks at the system that produced what happened to you. The forty-hour week. The retirement promise. The healthcare tether. Not to generate bitterness — but because you cannot build a strategy to protect yourself from something you have not fully seen. You need to acknowledge first, before you learn from it.

Part Three stabilizes you. The financial triage. The legal reality. The identity work of figuring out who you are when the role is stripped away.

Part Four repositions you. The shift from employee thinking to strategic thinking. The honest conversation about age and risk. The map of thirteen specific paths forward.

Part Five builds the foundation that makes sure this never corners you again.

Each chapter ends with Honest Reflections — questions designed not to be answered quickly, but to be sat with. Some of them will be uncomfortable. That is intentional. The discomfort is the work.

— — —

One more thing before you turn the page.

You did not fail.

The model did.

The company that removed you was operating exactly as it was designed to operate. It saw a cost. It made a calculation. It executed efficiently and without malice.

That does not make it right. It makes it a system — one that was never fully built for you, and one that you now have the opportunity to stop building for.

What you build instead is what this book is about.

Let's begin.

PART I The Hit

Chapter 1: Spat-Out and Shocked

The meeting was scheduled without warning.

No subject line that prepared you.

No context in the calendar invite.

Just a room, a time, and the quiet feeling that something was wrong.

I had been with the company for five years.

Process auditor. Process improvement director. A role that required me to be everywhere — sixty percent of my time on planes, in airports, in conference rooms across the country and around the world. I had given that company my schedule, my weekends, my presence in cities far from home. I had flown through delays, rescheduled dinners, and missed things I can't get back.

I was good at what I did.

I knew it. They knew it.

And then came the meeting.

— — —

I had a feeling something was shifting. You develop instincts after enough years in corporate environments. You read the room before you walk into it. You notice who isn't copied on emails. You sense the change in temperature before anyone names it.

So when they told me my position was being eliminated — that the company was looking for ways to "make up a shortfall" due to improperly built projections and forecasts — I wasn't completely blindsided.

But here's what I didn't expect.

It still hit.

Hard.

Not because I didn't see it coming. But because knowing something is possible and living through it are two entirely different things. There is no intellectual preparation that fully cushions the moment someone tells you that your role — the thing you organized your life around — is gone.

I walked out of that room and called my wife.

— — —

She answered on the second ring.

I told her what happened. Not in a composed, structured way. Just the facts, delivered with the kind of controlled calm that you perform when you're actually anything but calm underneath.

"We have savings. I know you're going to be shocked and angry. But we're going to be okay."

She was right.

And I knew she was right.

But knowing you're going to be okay and feeling okay are not the same thing.

— — —

The hardest part wasn't the meeting.

It wasn't the walk to the car, or the phone call, or telling people who needed to know.

The hardest part was the days that followed.

The texts from colleagues who heard.

The calls from managers and directors who found out and reached out with the professional version of condolences.

The constant performance of being fine.

I was not fine.

I was pissed.

Not panicked — but angry in the way that you get angry when you've given something everything and the thing doesn't care. When you've rearranged your life around a company's needs and the company reduces you to a line item in a cost-cutting conversation.

"Making up a shortfall due to improperly built projections."

Let that sentence sit for a second.

The company built flawed projections. The company made forecasting errors. And the solution to those errors was eliminating people who had nothing to do with building them.

I didn't mismanage their finances.

I didn't build the bad projections.

I showed up. Traveled. Delivered.

And yet.

— — —

Here is what I want you to understand, before we go any further.

This was not my first time being spat out.

About ten years earlier, I had lost a job at a company where I didn't get along with the owner. That exit was different. Messier. More personal in some ways. And at that point in my life, I had no savings to speak of. No position. No cushion between me and the edge.

I panicked then.

Completely.

The fear was immediate, physical, consuming. I wasn't thinking about what was next. I was thinking about what was now — the bills, the obligations, the gap between income and everything that required income to function.

That kind of panic doesn't leave room for clarity.

It doesn't leave room for strategy.

It doesn't leave room for anything except survival.

This time was different.

Not because the hit wasn't real. Not because the anger wasn't real.

But because the position was different.

My wife had a strong career. We had built savings — not because we were wealthy, but because we had been intentional. We had created distance between ourselves and the edge of the cliff. Not a lot of distance. But enough.

Enough to breathe.

And breathing — real breathing, not the shallow kind you do when fear is running your math — changes everything.

— — —

I remember sitting with my wife and telling her what I felt.

Not just the anger. Not just the disbelief. But the thing underneath both of those — the thing that surprised me.

I didn't panic.

After everything — five years of travel, of investment, of performance — being removed from a role by someone else's flawed spreadsheet should have sent me into a spiral.

It didn't.

Because we had built position before we needed it.

In my first book, The Leverage Code, I wrote about the difference between operating from need and operating from position. When you need the job, you accept things. You stay quiet. You overextend. Not because you lack strength — but because you lack insulation.

When you have position — savings, options, a partner with income, a cushion between you and collapse — you respond differently. You still feel the hit. But you don't collapse under it.

That night, talking to my wife, I made a decision.

I was going to write about this.

Not just the mechanics of what happened — the corporate math, the merger logic, the way companies erase people without erasing their own profitability. But the experience of it. The anger. The phone calls. The performance of being fine when you're not.

And most importantly — why some people get spat out and spiral, while others get spat out and eventually, quietly, build something better.

The difference is rarely talent.

It is almost always position.

— — —

This book is called SPAT-OUT because that is exactly what it feels like.

You give years — sometimes decades — to a company. You travel. You sacrifice. You produce. You show up in ways that don't make it into any performance review.

And then one day, in a ten-minute meeting, the company chews through those years and spits you out.

Not with malice.

Not even with awareness.

Just math.

The term is blunt. It's meant to be.

Because the experience is blunt. And the people who've lived it deserve a book that doesn't soften it with corporate language or dress it up in optimism before it earns that optimism.

You were spat out.

That happened.

And it matters — not just financially, but psychologically, structurally, and at the level of identity. Because for most people, the job isn't just income. It's schedule, purpose, community, and a significant piece of how we answer the question: who am I?

When the job disappears, that question becomes urgent in a way it rarely was before.

— — —

We are going to work through all of it in this book.

Not in a linear, everything-is-going-to-be-fine way. But in an honest, eyes-open way that respects what you've been through while refusing to let you stay there.

We'll start where most books won't — with what the corporate system was actually designed to do, and why your loyalty was never part of that design. Not because you need to be angry at the system forever, but because understanding the system clearly is the first step to stop being surprised by it.

Then we'll move through the stabilization phase — the financial triage, the legal reality, the identity work of figuring out who you are when the title is gone.

And then we'll rebuild.

Not back into the same cage. Not into the same system that just demonstrated it doesn't protect you. But into something more deliberate, more resilient, and built on a foundation that no single employer can pull out from under you.

By the end of this book, you will have a framework for building leverage — real leverage, the invisible kind that changes how you breathe in the hard moments — so that the next time disruption comes, and it will come, you are not standing at the edge of a cliff.

You are standing on ground you built yourself.

— — —

But first — let's talk about what just happened to you.

Because before strategy, there must be honesty.

And the honest truth is this:

You didn't fail.

The model did.

And once you understand the difference between those two things, everything that comes next becomes possible.

— — —

What Happened After the Meeting

My wife had a plan before I even fully processed what had happened.

We were going to get massages. Then go for a walk.

It sounds almost too simple. And in the moment, some part of me resisted it — the part that wanted to sit with the anger, to let it metabolize into something useful, to go straight to the desk and start figuring out the next move. That is who I am. Get shit done. Find the problem, fix the problem, move forward.

But she was right to insist.

The massage forced a physical release of something I had been holding tighter than I realized. The walk gave us space to talk — not about strategy, not about money, not about what comes next. Just to talk. About what happened. About how it felt. About the gap between having anticipated something and actually living through it.

Because those are not the same thing.

I had known something was shifting. I had prepared — financially, emotionally, conversationally. My wife and I had already discussed the possibility weeks before the meeting happened. We had looked at our runway. We had had the hard conversations about what we would do if the income stopped.

And still. When it actually happened — when the meeting was over and I was in the car and the badge was deactivated and five years of airports and deliverables and sixty-percent travel was suddenly just gone — it hit in a way that preparation does not fully prevent.

The massage helped. The walk helped. The ability to say out loud, to the person who mattered most, exactly what I was feeling without managing the presentation of it — that helped most of all.

If I had been alone in this, the story would have been different.

Without my wife, without the position we had built together, without the runway that gave us room to breathe rather than scramble — I know exactly what I would have done. Gone home. Watched television for a week. Then sat at the computer applying to every job I could find that paid enough to survive. Not thinking about building something. Not thinking about turning curiosity into income. Just trying to replace the paycheck as quickly as possible.

That version of the story ends in a different place.

Position is not just financial. It is the difference between a crisis that forces you into the first available exit and a difficulty that gives you room to choose the right one.

— — —

The Manager Who Left a Month Earlier

There was one colleague I called in those first days. A manager I had been close with — someone who had been in the trenches with me, who understood the industry in the specific way that comes from having operated inside it rather than observed it.

He had resigned about a month before I was let go.

We talked. We discussed the state of the company, the direction things had been moving, the feeling that something structural was shifting in ways that the official communications were not acknowledging. He had seen it too. That was partly why he had left.

What we did not discuss — what I wish, in retrospect, we had spent more time on — was what I was going to do next. Not the job search. The build. The specific question of what someone with my background and skills could construct independently, outside the structures that had contained both of us for years.

I did not have that conversation because I had not fully framed the question yet. The loss of the job clarified it in ways that being employed had obscured. When you are inside the structure, the structure answers the question of what you are doing with your time. When the structure disappears, the question becomes urgent.

What I did have, even in those first days, was the beginning of an answer.

I had always wanted to write books. The Leverage Code had been inside me for years — the framework I had been teaching informally in every coaching conversation, every whiteboard session with a struggling manager, every slow-season conversation about what it meant to build position before you needed it. The layoff did not create the desire to write. It removed the excuse not to.

And it added new material. This book exists because of what happened in that ten-minute meeting.

Honest Reflections

> *When the news landed, what was your first instinct — call someone, go quiet, get angry, go numb? What does that reaction tell you about how you're built?*
>
> *Did you see it coming? If yes, why didn't you act on that instinct earlier? If no, what story were you telling yourself that kept you from seeing it?*
>
> *How much of your daily identity — your sense of purpose, structure, and self-worth — was tied to that role? What's left standing without it?*

What did you give to that company that didn't show up in any performance review? Is that something you're willing to give to a system that wasn't built to protect you again?

If a close friend described exactly what happened to you — same circumstances, same tenure, same outcome — what would you tell them? Are you telling yourself the same thing?

Chapter 2: The Spiral — Shame, Anger, and the Ego Collapse

Nobody tells you about the performance.

Not the performance review that preceded the meeting.

Not the performance metrics they cited when they needed you.

The performance after.

The one where you answer the phone with a steady voice when your former colleague calls to say they heard. Where you describe what happened with just enough calm to signal that you're fine. Where you choose your words carefully — not because you're lying, exactly, but because the full truth feels too exposed.

That performance is exhausting.

And almost nobody talks about it.

— — —

Here's what I knew about layoffs before mine.

I knew the official language. Restructuring. Reduction in force. Role elimination.

I also knew what people actually thought when they heard someone was gone.

Because I had thought it too.

Every time a colleague disappeared — no announcement, just suddenly absent from the calendar, the email threads, the group chat — there was a quiet calculation that happened in my head.

What did he do?

Did he finally get caught at something?

Did he mess up a project? Get into it with his boss?

We tell ourselves we're just curious. That we're piecing together information. That it's not judgment.

It is judgment.

And I knew — the moment I walked out of that meeting — that the same calculation was happening about me.

That's the part they don't prepare you for.

Not the financial shock. Not the logistical scramble.

The quiet, private shame of knowing that people who respect you are now running the same mental math you once ran about others. Wondering what you did. What you missed. What finally caught up with you.

Even when you know — logically, clearly — that you did nothing wrong.

Even when you understand the corporate math better than most.

It still lands.

— — —

I want to be honest about something.

I'm over fifty.

That changes the calculation in ways that are hard to explain to someone younger.

When you're in your twenties or thirties, a job loss hits your reputation like a threat. Your brand is still being built. Your credibility is still being established. The fear is: what will people think of me? Will this follow me?

By the time you've been in an industry for decades, that particular fear softens.

I wasn't going to "lose followers."

What I was going to lose was something quieter and, in some ways, harder to replace.

The colleagues who knew how brutal the industry actually was. The managers who had been in the trenches with me. The people who spoke the same language — not corporate language, but the real language. The shorthand that develops between people who've survived the same pressure, solved the same problems, been in the same impossible rooms.

That community doesn't transfer easily.

You can't LinkedIn your way back into it immediately. You can't recreate in six months what took years to build. The professional friendships, the mutual credibility, the sense of shared context — that's what a layoff quietly dismantles alongside the paycheck.

And that loss is more personal than most people admit.

— — —

Two weeks before it happened to me, I was in a room where they discussed cutting management payroll by twelve percent.

I knew the math.

I knew who was going to be "reduced" before they did.

I sat with that knowledge and I thought what almost everyone thinks in that moment:

At least it's not me.

Two weeks later, it was me.

There is something uniquely clarifying about that experience — about having watched the machine operate from the inside, believing yourself protected by your visibility and your performance, and then discovering that the machine does not actually see you the way you see yourself.

It sees cost.

It sees headcount.

It sees line items that can be reduced to improve a ratio.

Your performance, your tenure, your institutional knowledge — those are factors in a different calculation. One that the finance team runs differently than you'd like to believe.

I don't say this to be bitter.

I say it because understanding it is the only thing that releases you from the self-blame spiral that follows almost every layoff.

The spiral that sounds like:

What did I do wrong?

Why me specifically?

Was there a sign I missed?

Could I have done something differently?

The answer, in most restructurings, is no.

You weren't targeted. You were calculated.

Those are not the same thing.

— — —

Let's talk about the ego.

Not the arrogant kind. The functional kind — the self-image you've built over a career, the internal story you carry about who you are in professional settings.

I had spent years traveling sixty percent of the time. Airports. Conference rooms. Cities that blurred into each other. The rhythm of a life built around being needed somewhere. Being the person who flew in to assess, improve, direct. The one organizations called when something needed to be fixed.

That identity doesn't survive a layoff without taking damage.

Even when you know it's not about your capability. Even when you've seen enough of how the system works to understand exactly what happened.

Something still cracks.

And I will tell you what I was not willing to show in those phone calls and texts.

That crack.

I didn't want to seem stressed. I didn't want to seem weak. I didn't want them to see me sweat.

There's something particular about the way men — or at least, the way I was conditioned — carry professional identity. You don't show the wound. You manage the image. You perform composure so naturally that after a while, you're not sure where the performance ends and the actual feeling begins.

"I knew it was coming," I told some people. "So it wasn't really a shock."

That was true. And it wasn't true.

I told my wife the real version. Everyone else got the edited one — the version where I had anticipated it, processed it, and was already moving forward.

What I was actually doing was protecting my image.

My pride was hurt. Not shattered — but dinged. The kind of ding you feel when you reach for the confidence that's usually there and find something slightly less solid underneath.

I wouldn't let them see me sweat while working. Why should they see it now?

Looking back, I can see it for what it was: a coping mechanism, not a weakness. The performance of composure isn't dishonest. It's protective. It buys you time to process in private what you're not ready to process in public.

But it has a cost.

When you perform composure for everyone except the person closest to you, the emotional weight accumulates quietly. The calls. The texts. The careful calibration of each response. The energy it takes to manage your image while simultaneously managing the actual disorientation of losing a structure you'd organized your life around.

That energy has to come from somewhere.

And it comes from the same reserves you need for what comes next.

— — —

The spiral started to slow when my wife said something simple.

"We got this. We have savings. We can go visit family now. Go to Fiji. Go for long walks. Sleep until nine in the morning."

It sounds almost too simple to be the turning point.

But something shifted when she said it.

Not because it erased the anger, or the sting, or the work of rebuilding. But because it pointed in a direction.

Forward.

It showed a future.

And this is something I believe deeply, having watched what happens to people when they're spat out:

Hope is not soft. Hope is structural.

When someone can see a future — even an imperfect, uncertain, still-being-built future — they make better decisions. They move toward something. They think in terms of months and years, not just days.

When someone cannot see a future, the math changes entirely.

Desperation sets in. Impulsiveness follows. Decisions get made from panic rather than position — and decisions made from panic almost always extend the damage rather than limit it.

I have watched people take the first job offered to them out of fear, only to find themselves in a worse situation two years later than if they had paused.

I have watched people burn bridges during the spiral — sending emails they can't unsend, making calls they can't take back — because they were operating from a place of no hope.

I have watched people disappear into the shame of it, contracting their world down to the size of their humiliation, cutting off the very relationships and opportunities that could have moved them forward.

None of that is weakness. All of it is the predictable outcome of operating without hope — without the ability to see that a future exists beyond the current pain.

My wife gave me a future in that moment.

A small one. Fiji and long walks and sleeping late. But it was direction. It was the first evidence that life on the other side of this was not only survivable but potentially, surprisingly, good.

That's when the spiral started to slow.

Not because the circumstances had changed.

Because the horizon had appeared.

— — —

And then something else happened.

Once the blow softened enough — not gone, not resolved, just softened — my brain didn't move toward rest.

It moved toward action.

I started thinking about what I could do. Not what I needed to do. Not what I was obligated to scramble toward. What I could do.

I could write a book. Maybe two. Maybe three.

I could build content. Start creating on social media in a real, deliberate way — not the passive scrolling of someone consuming, but the active output of someone building.

I could go deep on AI tools. Use them seriously, as a writer and creator, not just dabble. Turn that curiosity into a real skill set.

I could start moving again — physically, creatively, strategically. Just move.

I have always been an action person.

Not reckless action. Not panic-driven scrambling. But the kind of forward motion that is, for some people, the only thing that actually works. The kind where you don't wait until you feel ready, because feeling ready is a myth. You move, and the motion itself generates the clarity.

I want to be careful here, because this is not a universal prescription.

Some people need to sit with the loss before they can act. They need the grief to complete itself before strategy makes any sense. If that's you, honor that. The spiral has its own timeline and forcing action before you're ready can be its own form of avoidance.

But for the action-oriented — for the people who are already, somewhere in the back of their minds, thinking about moves while they're still managing the shock — I want to say this directly:

That instinct is not denial. It is recovery.

The pivot from what just happened to me to what can I do next is not skipping the grief. It is the grief transforming. It is the moment your mind decides, not consciously but viscerally, that you are going to build something from this rather than be buried by it.

Pay attention to that moment when it comes.

It arrives differently for everyone. For me it came through my wife's words, and then through the quiet mental inventory of possibilities — the books, the content, the tools, the motion.

When it arrives for you, don't dismiss it as too soon or too optimistic.

It's the spiral breaking.

It's the strategist inside you waking up.

Let it.

Because the best revenge is success.

— — —

The spiral is normal.

The shame, the anger, the ego damage, the performance of composure — all of it is normal. It is what happens when something you organized your identity around is removed without your consent. It would be stranger if none of that happened.

But the spiral is not permanent.

And it does not have to be extended by the decisions you make inside it.

The single most important thing you can do in the first days and weeks after a layoff is this:

Find the horizon.

It doesn't have to be Fiji. It doesn't have to be dramatic or transformational. It just has to be something in the future that you can see and move toward. A conversation you're going to have. A trip you've been putting off. A project that has nothing to do with work. A morning where you don't set an alarm.

Something that tells your nervous system: there is a future here, and it is livable.

Because everything in this book — the strategy, the rebuilding, the leverage — requires a functioning mind to execute. And a mind trapped in a spiral, operating from shame or fear or the performance of being fine, is not yet at full capacity.

Give it something to move toward.

Even something small.

The strategy can wait a few days.

The horizon cannot.

— — —

Once you can feel the shift from reactive to something steadier — we need to look at something most people would rather avoid.

The system that built the machine that spat you out.

Not to assign blame.

But to understand exactly how it works.

Because you cannot protect yourself from something you don't fully see.

And once you see it clearly, you will never be surprised by it again.

— — —

Day Three

I gave myself two days.

Day one was the massage and the walk and the talking. Day two was quieter — the anger still present but no longer sharp, the shock settling into something more like a sustained low-frequency hum. I watched some television. I ate meals at times that made sense. I let the stillness be what it was.

Day three, I ate breakfast, went to my home office, and opened a browser.

I typed: how to write a book using AI.

I spent six hours down that path. ChatGPT. Amazon KDP. Publishing costs. Pro plan features and what the price difference actually bought. I was not dabbling — I was researching with the same systematic approach I had applied to operational problems for thirty years. Map the terrain. Understand the costs. Identify the decision points. Build the plan.

I spent three days doing nothing but that. Then my wife suggested a walk. Then three more days at the desk. Then a computer game — about four hours of it, which felt necessary and slightly guilty in equal measure.

And then something happened.

Something in the back of my head started nagging.

Not guilt, exactly. Not anxiety. Something more like urgency — the specific sensation of knowing that work was waiting and that sitting away from it was costing something. Not money. Time. The finite, non-recoverable kind.

I put the game down and went back to the desk.

That moment — the nagging, the pull back to the work — was the spiral breaking. Not because the circumstances had changed. Because the part of my brain that is wired for action had identified what the action was. And once it had identified it, it would not stop pointing at it.

Get shit done.

That is not just a motto. It is the operating system. And the operating system had found its task.

— — —

What the Anger Was Actually About

I need to say something about the anger more honestly than I have so far.

The anger was real. But what it was about was not entirely what it appeared to be about.

On the surface, it was about the meeting. The clinical efficiency of it. The ten minutes. The HR language. The way five years of travel and delivery and institutional investment was wrapped into a sentence about "making up a shortfall due to improperly built projections."

That was real. And it was legitimate.

But underneath it was something I had to sit with more carefully.

I am someone who fixes things. That is not a professional description — it is a personal one. I find the broken thing, I understand why it is broken, I build the system that makes it work. That is what I do in a building, in a relationship, with a piece of equipment, with a struggling manager who cannot figure out why their team is not executing. I fix things. I get things done. I move forward.

The layoff put me in a situation I could not fix. There was no conversation to have, no process to improve, no lever to pull that would change the outcome. The decision had been made by people I did not know, based on numbers I had not built, for reasons that had nothing to do with the quality of my work.

For someone whose identity is built around solving problems and producing results, that is a specific kind of infuriating.

Not because of the title. Not because of the status. Because of the inability to do anything about it.

I had to calm myself down internally more than once in those first days. Not for performance. For myself. Because the anger, if I had let it run, would have consumed the energy I needed for what came next. And I knew — even in the middle of it — that what came next was more important than what had just happened.

The best revenge is success. I have believed that for a long time. In those first days, I was holding onto it like a handle.

— — —

The Traction Problem

I want to say something honest that most books about reinvention skip entirely.

The hardest part is not the beginning.

The beginning has urgency and adrenaline and the clarity that comes from having just had everything stripped away. The beginning has the massage and the walk and day three at the desk with a new purpose. The beginning has the anger converted into fuel and the plan taking shape and the first actions producing the first evidence that something is being built.

The hardest part is the middle. The weeks and months when the work is happening consistently but the traction has not yet arrived. When you are on your third book and the first two have not yet found the audience they are meant to find. When you are posting, creating, building — and the numbers are still small and the sales are still quiet and the results that your entire professional identity has always been calibrated around are not yet visible.

I will tell you where I am right now, honestly.

I am in the middle.

I am not standing on the cliff. The runway exists. The work is real. The optimism is genuine rather than performed. But I am not patient by nature — I expect results, from others and from myself, and the absence of traction after sustained effort is a specific kind of difficult that no one prepares you for adequately.

Traction, for me, equals results. And I have not seen the results yet.

I include this not to discourage you. I include it because the honest version of this story is still in progress — and you deserve a book written by someone who is inside the experience, not one who has already arrived at the comfortable ending and is describing the journey from safety.

The spiral does not end neatly. It slows, and then it starts moving in the other direction, and then it stalls again, and then it builds. That is what the real version looks like.

And the real version is survivable.

Because the alternative — going back to the hot stove, rebuilding the same fragile structure, trading the possibility of something you own for the certainty of something that can be revoked in ten minutes — is worse.

I would rather be in the middle of building something real than at the beginning of another arrangement that ends the same way.

The spiral is worth it.

Keep going.

Honest Reflections

> *When the calls and texts came in, who did you tell the real story to — and who got the edited version? What were you protecting?*
>
> *Where did the shame come from? Was it about what people would think — or about what you were afraid it said about you?*
>
> *Have you allowed yourself to actually be angry — not managed, not performed, but genuinely angry? If not, where is it going?*
>
> *Can you see a horizon yet? Not a plan — just a direction. A possibility. Something on the other side of this that feels livable. If not, what is blocking it?*
>
> *Are you an action person or a process person when it comes to recovery? Be honest — not*

> *about who you think you should be, but about how you actually move through hard things.*
>
> *What is the first move — not the right move, not the perfect move, just the first one — that your gut is already telling you to make?*

Chapter 3: Loyalty Is Dead — Mergers, Models, and the Math

Karen had been with the company for seventeen years.

She started as a project analyst and worked her way up to Director of Operations. She was the person leadership called when something needed to be fixed — not managed, not monitored, but actually fixed. Her name carried weight. Her track record was real.

So when the email hit her inbox — subject line: Urgent: Business Update Meeting — she didn't panic. She'd been in plenty of updates. She assumed she'd be leading part of the conversation.

Instead, she sat across from a VP she barely knew and an HR rep who read from a script.

The company was merging with a former competitor. There was "role duplication." Her position was being eliminated.

Her face went numb.

She asked one question: "Was there something I did wrong?"

The HR rep replied: "This has nothing to do with performance."

That was both true and cruel.

Karen's badge deactivated by five o'clock.

— — —

Karen's story is not unusual.

It is the story of tens of thousands of people every year — competent, committed, long-tenured professionals who gave everything to an organization and discovered, in a ten-minute meeting, that the organization had been running a different calculation the entire time.

Not a calculation about performance.

About cost.

About headcount.

About what two companies look like when you lay them on top of each other and start circling the redundancies.

Understanding that calculation — clearly, without flinching — is not cynicism.

It is the most important piece of career intelligence you can carry.

Because you cannot protect yourself from a system you refuse to see.

— — —

What Mergers Actually Promise

When two companies announce a merger, there is a public story and a private one.

The public story is about growth. Market expansion. Combined strengths. Synergies that will make both organizations more competitive.

The private story — the one told in boardrooms and investor calls — is about cost.

Specifically: how much of it can be eliminated.

When executives present a merger to shareholders, they almost always highlight expected cost synergies. That phrase is the corporate language for a straightforward reality: we plan to cut overlapping jobs, consolidate functions, and reduce payroll to improve the bottom line.

The language is designed to sound strategic.

The outcome is structural.

Two HR departments become one. Two marketing leads become one. Two layers of operations, two regional directors, two project management offices — the model looks at each pairing and asks a simple question:

Can we do this with one instead of two?

Almost always, the answer is yes.

And when the answer is yes, someone goes home.

— — —

The Language They Use to Move You Out

There is a vocabulary built specifically for this moment.

You will hear words like: operational efficiency. Streamlined leadership. Consolidation of roles. Labor optimization. Elimination of redundancies.

Each phrase is engineered to accomplish two things simultaneously: describe a financial decision and remove the human being from the sentence.

"Role duplication" sounds like an organizational problem.

It is a person.

"Labor optimization" sounds like a process improvement.

It is someone's career.

"Elimination of redundancies" sounds like efficiency.

It is Karen. It is Daniel. It is you.

The language exists to make the decision feel inevitable and impersonal — which, from the organization's perspective, it is. But for the person receiving it, it is neither inevitable nor impersonal. It is a life-altering event delivered in the vocabulary of a spreadsheet.

Don't let the language confuse you about what actually happened.

You weren't optimized.

You were cut.

— — —

No Level Is Safe

One of the most dangerous beliefs in corporate life is that seniority is protection.

It isn't.

In many restructurings, senior leaders — VPs, Directors, C-suite lieutenants — are the first to go. Not because they failed, but because they are expensive. And because the acquiring company often brings their own people into those seats. Familiarity and financial alignment, not fairness, determine who stays.

Junior employees aren't safe either. Entry-level programs get paused or scrapped entirely. Contractors are released. Internal mobility freezes. Raises get delayed or quietly canceled.

Consider three people caught in the same merger:

A director with seventeen years of tenure — gone because her role duplicated a position the acquiring company already had filled.

A mid-level manager whose entire team was absorbed into a centralized department three states away.

A new hire who received a call two days before her start date. "Change in business conditions," they said.

Three different tenures. Three different levels. One result.

The model didn't make space for any of them.

No level on the org chart is immune. The sooner you internalize that, the sooner you stop building your security on the wrong foundation.

— — —

What the Model Actually Measures

Here is what executives are actually looking at when they run a post-merger integration model:

Cost per employee relative to output. Labor ratios — headcount against revenue. Organizational layers — how many levels of management exist between the front line and the executive suite. Span of control — how many direct reports each manager carries. Overhead — office space, administrative functions, support roles.

Nowhere in that model is there a field for years of service.

Nowhere is there a calculation for institutional knowledge.

Nowhere does it ask: how many crises did this person prevent? How many problems did they solve before anyone else knew they existed? How many people did they develop, retain, and protect?

Those things are real. They matter enormously to the day-to-day functioning of an organization.

They do not fit in the model.

And what doesn't fit in the model doesn't factor into the decision.

That is not a moral failure on the part of the people running the model. It is a limitation of the tool. But it is a limitation that costs real people real livelihoods.

Understanding this is not about bitterness.

It is about clarity.

The model is not evil. It is incomplete.

And you were never going to win an argument with an incomplete model by working harder.

— — —

Loyalty Is a Feeling. Cuts Are a Function.

For decades, the employment contract — written and unwritten — promised something like this:

Show up. Work hard. Be loyal. Build tenure. And the company will take care of you.

That contract is gone.

Not recently gone. Not gone because of any single recession or industry shift. Gone structurally, systematically, over the course of several decades, as the balance of power between employer and employee was quietly rewritten in favor of the employer.

The 401(k) replaced the pension. Benefits became contingent rather than guaranteed. Job security became a performance metric rather than a cultural commitment. And loyalty — the thing employees gave freely and completely — became a one-sided transaction.

You were loyal to the company.

The company was loyal to its margins.

Those are not the same relationship.

Loyalty is an emotion. It lives in people. It drives behavior — the extra hours, the covered shifts, the problems solved on weekends, the ideas contributed that made someone else look good.

Corporate cuts are a function. They live in spreadsheets. They are driven by ratios and targets and the quarterly pressure to demonstrate financial discipline to people who will never know your name.

Confusing the two is not just a mistake.

It is the mistake that leaves people most blindsided when the meeting comes.

You can be the most loyal person in the building and still be the first name on the list. Not because loyalty is worthless. But because the list was never measuring loyalty.

— — —

Pain Is an Accelerant

There is a particular kind of pain that comes from being removed from a role you gave your best years to.

It hits differently than failure.

Because it isn't failure. That's what makes it so disorienting. You didn't fail. You were functioning, contributing, delivering — and then you were gone. The ground moved, not your performance.

That pain is real. Don't rush past it.

But don't stay in it either.

Because pain, when you let it do its job, does something useful: it burns away the illusions.

The illusion that loyalty is protection.

The illusion that performance guarantees permanence.

The illusion that the company sees you the way you see yourself.

Once those illusions are gone, something clearer takes their place.

You begin to see the system for what it actually is — not built to protect you, but to generate returns. And once you see that, clearly and without resentment, you can make a different kind of decision.

Not about what the company owes you.

About what you owe yourself.

The strategist in you doesn't emerge despite the pain.

It emerges because of it.

— — —

The Numbers Behind the Cuts

Here is what the data actually shows about how corporations use layoffs — not the story told in press releases, but the pattern visible in the numbers.

Between 2018 and 2024, major U.S. corporations announced hundreds of thousands of layoffs in years where they simultaneously reported record profits. Technology companies that cut tens of thousands of workers in 2022 and 2023 had, in many cases, spent the previous two years buying back their own stock — a mechanism that enriches shareholders and executives whose compensation is tied to share price, while reducing the workforce that produced the profits that made the buybacks possible.

This is not a coincidence. It is the system functioning as designed.

The pressure on publicly traded companies to hit quarterly earnings targets is structural and relentless. When revenue projections miss — even slightly — the first lever executives reach for is headcount. Not because it is the most effective long-term strategy. Because it is the fastest way to move a cost number and show analysts that management is "taking action."

The workers who are cut are not the ones who built the bad projections. They are the ones whose salaries appear as a line item that can be reduced before the next earnings call.

You were a line item. That is not a metaphor. That is the accounting reality of how you appeared on the spreadsheet that produced your layoff.

— — —

What Loyalty Was Actually Worth

Corporate loyalty is one of the most successfully marketed fictions of the modern workplace.

The implicit contract went like this: give us your best years, your travel, your nights and weekends, your institutional knowledge, your professional identity — and in return, we will provide stability, advancement, and the security of belonging to something larger than yourself.

Most people believed it. Because for a period, it appeared to be true.

The stability was real — until it wasn't. The advancement was real — until the org chart changed. The security was real — until the merger, the acquisition, the quarterly shortfall, the new leadership team that arrived with its own relationships and its own priorities.

Loyalty, from the corporation's perspective, was never a two-way contract. It was a management tool. A way to extract maximum commitment from employees while retaining the flexibility to eliminate those employees the moment the financial calculation changed.

The research on this is consistent and has been for decades. Studies of corporate layoffs repeatedly find that long-tenured employees — the ones who stayed, who built institutional knowledge, who trained the next generation of managers — are disproportionately represented in layoff cohorts. Not because their performance was poor. Because their salaries, accumulated over years of raises, are higher than entry-level replacements. The loyalty premium becomes a liability on the balance sheet.

You were not naive to believe in the contract. You were responding rationally to signals the corporation sent deliberately. The performance reviews that said you were valued. The bonuses that confirmed it. The title progression that felt like evidence of a relationship.

Those signals were real. The contract behind them was not.

— — —

Executive Pay and the Math of Sacrifice

There is one more number worth sitting with.

In the same quarters when companies announce mass layoffs, executive compensation typically rises. The CEO who "made the hard decision" to cut ten percent of the workforce often receives a bonus for improving the cost structure. The CFO who found the efficiencies is rewarded with additional equity. The board that approved the reduction votes itself continued compensation.

Between 1978 and 2022, CEO compensation at major U.S. corporations grew by over 1,400 percent. Worker compensation grew by approximately 18 percent over the same period — barely keeping pace with inflation.

This is not presented here to generate anger, though anger is a reasonable response. It is presented because understanding the actual math of how corporate profits are distributed is the foundation of every strategic decision you make from this point forward.

When you understand that the system is designed to concentrate the upside at the top and distribute the risk throughout the workforce, you stop asking why loyalty was not rewarded. You start asking what you are going to build instead — and for whom.

The answer to that question is the rest of this book.

Honest Reflections

> *Did you believe — really believe — that your loyalty would protect you? Where did that belief come from?*

> *Looking back, were there signs that the company was running a different calculation than the one you assumed? What did you choose not to see?*
>
> *How much of your professional identity was built on your relationship with one employer? What would remain if that employer disappeared tomorrow?*
>
> *Have you been operating as an employee — waiting for the company to determine your value — or as a strategist, building position regardless of who signs your check?*
>
> *What would it mean for you, specifically, to stop being surprised by how the system works?*

— — —

The system is not going to change.

Mergers will keep happening. Models will keep running. Boards will keep rewarding the companies that cut decisively and report improved margins.

That is the reality.

The question is not whether the system will protect you.

It won't.

The question is what you are going to build that doesn't depend on it.

That conversation starts in the next chapter.

PART II The System That Was Never Built for You

Chapter 4: The 40-Hour Week Was Designed to Keep You Stuck

Before we talk about what you do next, we need to talk about the ground you've been standing on.

Because most people never stop to examine the structure beneath their working lives. They inherited it. They stepped into it. They organized their entire existence — their schedule, their identity, their financial planning, their relationship with time itself — around a framework they never chose and never questioned.

That framework was not built for you.

It was built for production.

And once you understand how it was actually constructed — and why — you will never look at a Monday morning the same way again.

— — —

Ford's Real Experiment

In 1926, Henry Ford did something that shocked the American manufacturing industry.

He cut his workers' schedule from six days a week — sometimes sixty hours — down to five days and forty hours, with no reduction in pay.

His competitors called it reckless. They predicted it would destroy productivity. They waited for Ford to fail.

Instead, output went up.

Ford had spent years studying the relationship between hours worked and actual productivity. What he found was straightforward: beyond a certain threshold, more hours produced diminishing returns. Workers made more mistakes. Quality dropped. The extra time on the clock wasn't generating extra value — it was generating fatigue.

Cutting hours, paradoxically, made the operation more efficient.

The rest of American industry eventually followed. And in 1938, the Fair Labor Standards Act codified what Ford had discovered — establishing the forty-hour week as the legal standard, with overtime required beyond it.

That is the official story. And it is true as far as it goes.

But there is more to it.

— — —

The Part of the Story That Gets Left Out

Ford was not purely motivated by worker well-being.

He was a businessman running a production machine. And he understood something that most people still don't examine closely enough: the forty-hour week was calibrated. Not just for maximum output — but for maximum containment.

Think about what forty hours a week actually does to a person's life.

Five days consumed. Two days returned.

Those two days — the weekend — were presented as a gift. Rest. Leisure. Time with family. Time to spend the wages you earned during the other five days.

Ford understood that workers needed to be consumers as well as producers. He famously wanted his own employees to be able to afford the cars they were building. The weekend wasn't just rest. It was shopping time. Spending time. Recovery time that prepared workers to return Monday and do it all over again.

The forty-hour week was not designed to give you freedom.

It was designed to give you just enough recovery to sustain your productivity — while leaving you just tired enough, and just occupied enough, that building something of your own remained out of reach.

Five days building someone else's dream.

Two days recovering from it.

Repeat for forty years.

That is not a life of freedom. That is a life of managed output.

— — —

The Post-War Lock-In

After World War II, millions of soldiers returned home.

The country needed to absorb them. Industry needed workers. And workers needed structure — income, purpose, a way to rebuild civilian life after years of war.

What emerged was a particular version of the American employment contract: show up, work hard, climb the ladder, and the system will take care of you. A pension at the end. Stability throughout. Security in exchange for loyalty.

For a generation of men who had survived genuine uncertainty, that contract was deeply appealing. It wasn't a trap. It felt like solid ground.

And for a time, it more or less held.

But it also created something else: a workforce psychologically organized around dependence. Around the expectation that the employer was the source of security. That loyalty would be rewarded. That the system, if you worked it faithfully, would deliver on its promises.

That expectation was passed down through generations.

Your parents may have inherited it. You almost certainly absorbed some version of it.

Work hard. Stay loyal. Don't rock the boat.

The system will take care of you.

You already know how that ended.

— — —

The Weekend as a Reward System

Pay attention to how the five-day week is talked about in everyday life.

"Thank God it's Friday."

"Just making it to the weekend."

"Two more days."

"I live for Saturdays."

We have organized our emotional relationship with time around the premise that five days are something to endure and two days are something to earn.

That is not a neutral relationship with your own life.

That is a framework in which the majority of your waking hours — the hours that make up the majority of your adult existence — are treated as the cost you pay to access the small portion that feels like yours.

When you spend most of your mental energy counting down to Friday, you are not living five days a week.

You are surviving them.

And the system counts on that.

A person focused on making it to the weekend does not have mental bandwidth to ask bigger questions. They don't have energy to build anything after hours. They don't have time to develop skills that might reduce their dependence on the employer.

The structure of the week produces the structure of the thinking.

Busy enough to be compliant. Tired enough to be contained.

That is not an accident.

— — —

The Healthcare Trap — How They Kept You Afraid to Leave

Of all the mechanisms built into the modern employment system, this one may be the most effective.

In 1942, the U.S. government froze wages to control wartime inflation. Employers couldn't compete for workers by raising salaries. So they found another way: benefits.

The War Labor Board ruled that health insurance contributions didn't count as wages under the freeze. So employers began offering health coverage to attract workers. It wasn't a philosophical commitment to employee well-being. It was a workaround.

Then in 1954, the tax code made it permanent. Employer contributions to health insurance became tax-exempt — making the arrangement attractive to both sides and locking it into the structure of American employment for generations.

The result: the United States became one of the only developed nations in the world where access to healthcare is tied directly to employment.

Think about what that means in practice.

It means that leaving a job — any job, no matter how toxic, how limiting, how misaligned with what you actually want to do with your life — carries a risk that workers in other countries simply don't face.

It means that the cost of your autonomy is, in part, your family's access to healthcare.

It means that the decision to take a risk, start something, walk away from something that isn't working — all of those decisions are complicated by a variable that has nothing to do with your professional capability or your financial readiness.

This was not an intentional conspiracy.

It was an accident of wartime policy that calcified into the dominant structure of American working life.

But the effect is the same, whether it was intentional or not.

It keeps people afraid to leave.

It makes the cost of sovereignty artificially high.

And it ensures that millions of people stay in roles they've outgrown, companies that don't value them, and systems that would spit them out without hesitation — because walking away means losing coverage for themselves and everyone who depends on them.

That is not a benefit.

That is a leash.

— — —

Your Best Years, Someone Else's Dreams

Here is the sentence from my notes that has stayed with me since the first time I read it years ago:

You spend your best years building someone else's dreams, not yours.

That is the compression of everything this chapter is about.

The forty-hour week. The weekend as reward. The healthcare tether. The post-war promise of stability that gradually became a system of managed dependence.

All of it designed — deliberately or accidentally, it barely matters — to keep your best energy, your best hours, your best years flowing toward someone else's enterprise.

And here is the part that makes this especially sharp for someone who has just been spat out:

You gave those years.

You gave the mornings and the late nights and the weekends when the project demanded it. You gave the energy that could have gone toward your own ideas, your own leverage, your own future.

And when the math changed — when the model updated, when the spreadsheet required a reduction — those years meant nothing to the calculation.

Not because your contribution wasn't real.

But because the system was never designed to remember it.

The forty-hour week was designed for production.

Healthcare was tied to employment by accident.

Loyalty was encouraged because it served the employer's interests.

None of it was designed for you.

Which means rebuilding — rebuilding correctly, not just finding the next version of the same cage —

requires building something the system was never going to hand you.

Your own leverage. Your own options. Your own position.

That is what the rest of this book is about.

Honest Reflections

> *Look honestly at your relationship with the work week. Were you living five days — or enduring them? What does that answer tell you about the life you were actually building?*
>
> *Has the fear of losing healthcare ever kept you in a role, a company, or a situation you wanted to leave? What did that cost you — beyond the financial calculation?*
>
> *How much of your professional energy over the past five or ten years went toward building your own leverage versus building someone else's enterprise? Does that ratio feel right to you?*
>
> *What would your working life look like if it were genuinely structured around your sovereignty — your time, your output, your terms? How far is that from what you have now?*
>
> *The post-war generation accepted the employment contract because it felt like solid*

> *ground. What contract are you willing to accept going forward — and what are you no longer willing to trade away?*

— — —

Understanding how the system was built does not mean you have to keep living inside it.

It means you can finally see it clearly enough to build something different.

The next chapter takes that further — into the promise of retirement, the disappearance of the pension, and what the system quietly decided you were no longer owed.

Chapter 5: Retirement Was a Carrot, Not a Promise

My father gave me one piece of financial advice that I never forgot.

He told me to put my money in real assets. Property. Things you could touch and own and that would hold value over time.

"Don't trust the stock market," he said. "It's a machine made for the rich, to benefit the rich, built on the pittance of the poor."

I was young enough to think he was being cynical.

He wasn't.

He had watched something happen to the American worker over the course of his working life — a slow, structural transfer of risk from the people who owned companies to the people who worked in them. A transfer so gradual and so carefully framed as progress that most people didn't recognize it for what it was until decades later, when the reality arrived in the form of a retirement account that wasn't enough, a market that had crashed at exactly the wrong time, and a finish line that kept moving further away.

That transfer had a name.

It was called the 401(k).

— — —

What a Pension Actually Was

Before we talk about what was taken, we need to understand what was there.

The pension — specifically the defined benefit pension — was a promise.

Not a possibility. Not a projection. A promise.

You worked for a company for a defined period of time. The company invested on your behalf. And when you retired, you received a guaranteed monthly payment for the rest of your life. The amount was predetermined. It did not depend on what the market did the year you retired. It did not require you to make investment decisions you had no training to make. It did not evaporate if a recession happened to hit at the wrong moment in your career.

The company carried the risk. You carried the work.

At the peak of the pension era, roughly half of all private sector workers in America had some form of defined benefit coverage. It was not universal. It was not perfect. But it was real — a structural commitment from the employer to the employee that extended beyond the last day of work.

That commitment had a cost.

And when corporations began to seriously feel that cost in the 1970s and 1980s — through market volatility, rising life expectancy, and the sheer weight of long-term obligations — they started looking for an exit.

They found one.

It was hiding in a line of the tax code.

— — —

The Accidental Revolution

In 1978, Congress passed the Revenue Act.

Section 401(k) was a minor provision — almost an afterthought — that allowed employees to defer a portion of their compensation on a pre-tax basis. It was originally designed to limit executive bonus deferral schemes. Nobody in Congress, by most accounts, intended to create the primary retirement savings vehicle for the entire American workforce.

But a benefits consultant named Ted Benna noticed something in the language.

He saw that 401(k) could be used to create a tax-advantaged savings plan for all employees — not just executives. He built the first such plan for his own company and began advocating for its adoption. The IRS signed off. Corporations took notice.

By the early 1980s, major companies were already beginning to see what the 401(k) offered them: a way to shift retirement responsibility from the balance sheet to the employee.

Pensions required companies to fund lifetime obligations. They required actuarial calculations, long-term investment management, and the guarantee that payments would continue no matter what the markets did.

The 401(k) required none of that.

Companies could contribute — or not. They could match a percentage — or change the match, or eliminate it, when times got tight. And when an employee was laid off? The obligation ended cleanly. No lifetime payout. No ongoing liability. Just whatever was in the account on the last day of employment.

For corporations, the calculus was simple.

The pension was messy and permanent.

The 401(k) was clean and finite.

By 1983, nearly half of all large firms were offering or considering a 401(k). The pension didn't die overnight. It was frozen, then defunded, then quietly replaced — generation by generation — with an account that put all the risk on the worker.

— — —

What the Transfer Actually Meant

Here is what the shift from pension to 401(k) actually transferred from employer to employee:

The investment risk. With a pension, the company managed the investments and guaranteed the outcome. With a 401(k), the employee chooses from a menu of funds and absorbs whatever the market delivers — including crashes, recessions, and the particular misfortune of retiring during a down year.

The decision-making burden. Most workers have no training in portfolio management. They are not investment professionals. They are people who worked in manufacturing, healthcare, logistics, management — and are now expected to make sophisticated financial decisions about asset allocation, risk tolerance, and withdrawal strategy. The system handed them a tool designed for specialists and called it freedom.

The political cover. By framing the 401(k) as "control" and "individual choice," the shift was sold as empowerment. You are in charge of your retirement now. This is better.

My father saw through that framing immediately.

"Investing your pittance in a machine built for the rich" is not empowerment. It is participation in someone else's wealth-building engine under the polite fiction that you are building your own.

The investment banks and hedge funds that manage 401(k) assets — that charge fees on every account, that benefit from the consistent inflow of worker contributions regardless of market performance — did not become less wealthy when the pension was replaced by the 401(k).

They became dramatically more so.

Because suddenly, millions of workers who had never before been participants in the stock market were required to be.

Not by choice.

By necessity.

— — —

The Clean Exit

There is one more dimension to this shift that almost never gets discussed openly.

The pension created friction when companies wanted to cut people.

A long-tenured employee with defined benefit coverage represented an ongoing financial obligation. Cutting them mid-career created complex actuarial questions – partial vesting, early payout triggers, legal obligations around the promised benefit.

The 401(k) eliminated all of that.

When you cut someone with a 401(k), the company's obligation ends the moment employment ends. Whatever is in the account is the employee's. Whatever the company was matching – that stops. Clean. Simple. Final.

No ongoing liability. No complicated payout calculations. No financial reason to think twice about a layoff.

The 401(k) didn't just shift retirement risk. It made the cost of cutting people lower.

And lower costs of cutting people means more cutting happens.

If you have ever wondered why layoffs seem to happen more casually than they once did – why a thirty-year employee can be walked out on a Tuesday with two weeks of severance and a handshake — this is part of the structural answer.

The financial architecture no longer discourages it.

— — —

What Other Countries Decided

The United States is nearly alone among developed nations in tying retirement security so completely to individual market participation.

Australia built a mandatory superannuation system in 1992. Every employer must contribute a percentage of every employee's earnings — currently twelve percent — directly into a retirement account. Not optional. Not subject to budget pressures. Mandatory. The employee doesn't have to remember to enroll. The employer doesn't have a choice about contributing.

Canada built the Canada Pension Plan — a mandatory, earnings-based pension covering virtually all workers, managed collectively, with benefits that do not rise and fall with the stock market.

The United Kingdom provides a state pension through National Insurance contributions, supplemented by mandatory workplace pension enrollment.

Most of Western Europe operates on variations of guaranteed state pension systems, with contributions required from both employers and employees throughout working life.

None of these systems are perfect. All of them have funding challenges, demographic pressures, and political debates about sustainability.

But all of them share one thing the American system largely abandoned in the 1980s:

The principle that retirement security is a shared obligation — not a personal investment challenge.

In the U.S., the working person was handed a brokerage account, told it was freedom, and wished good luck.

— — —

The Carrot

Here is the deeper truth underneath all of this.

Retirement was never simply a financial arrangement.

It was a motivational tool.

The promise of retirement — of security, comfort, and reward at the end of a working life — was the carrot that justified the forty-hour week, the decades of loyalty, the deferred gratification of putting off your own dreams in service of someone else's enterprise.

You endured Monday because of the promise of Friday.

You endured the career because of the promise of retirement.

That promise was real once — imperfect, unequal, but real.

Then the pension disappeared. The 401(k) arrived. The market crashed in 2001, again in 2008. People who had done everything right — contributed faithfully, stayed employed, planned carefully — watched their retirement accounts cut in half at exactly the moment they needed them most.

And the carrot moved.

The retirement age crept up. The savings required to retire comfortably grew. The math that once made retirement at 65 feasible became the math that makes retirement at 70 uncertain.

Over the past decade, the proportion of Americans working past the age of 65 has increased by sixty percent.

Not because they want to.

Because the promise wasn't kept.

— — —

My Father's Advice and What It Actually Means

My father gave me two pieces of wisdom that I carried my entire career.

The first was about the market: don't trust a machine built for the rich, to benefit the rich, on the pittance of the poor.

The second was about work itself.

"Only business owners get rich. When you work for someone, you help them get rich."

Read that again.

Not as cynicism. As arithmetic.

Every hour you invest in someone else's company compounds their equity, their revenue, their valuation — not yours. Every problem you solve, every relationship you build, every system you improve adds to their asset. You receive a salary. They receive the accumulation.

The retirement promise was, at its core, the system's answer to that arithmetic. It said: yes, you are building our wealth. But stay long enough, stay loyal enough, and we will take care of you at the end.

That was the deal.

The pension was the proof the deal was real.

When the pension disappeared, the deal was broken. The company kept the equity you helped build. You kept an account that moved with the market and a retirement age that kept shifting out of reach.

My father saw it coming before most people were willing to name it.

The retirement promise was not real.

It was the story that kept you working.

And the people who got genuinely wealthy — the ones who didn't need the promise to hold — were the ones who owned something. Who built something. Who had equity in what they created rather than a claim on what they were told they'd receive someday.

This is not a call to quit your job tomorrow.

It is a call to stop organizing your entire financial future around a promise that the last fifty years have demonstrated cannot be relied upon.

Build real assets. Property. Skills. Multiple income streams. Businesses you own. Content that generates revenue whether you're working that day or not.

These are not just investment strategies.

They are the difference between being someone who helped another person get rich and being someone who built something for themselves.

And that refusal — building position before you need it, building leverage before it's demanded — is exactly what this book is asking you to do.

The carrot was never guaranteed.

But the work you do on your own terms?

Nobody can rewrite the projections on that.

— — —

Honest Reflections

> *Did you ever genuinely believe retirement was guaranteed — or did some part of you always sense it was shakier than advertised? What were you choosing not to examine?*
>
> *How much of your working life has been structured around a retirement promise that the system has quietly renegotiated without your consent? What would you do differently if you started over today?*

> *Look at your current retirement picture honestly. Is it a position of strength — or are you more dependent on market performance and continued employment than you're comfortable admitting?*
>
> *Beyond a retirement account, what assets do you actually own or control? What generates value for you independent of who's paying your salary?*
>
> *What would it mean to build a financial life that doesn't require a corporation to keep its promises? What is the first move in that direction that you've been putting off?*

— — —

The system was never fully built for your retirement.

It was built for your productivity — and retirement was the story told to sustain it.

Now that you see the story clearly, the next chapter turns to something more immediate: how the same system that controlled your time and outsourced your retirement also made sure you were afraid to leave.

And what it looks like to stop being afraid.

Chapter 6: Health Benefits, Golden Handcuffs, and the Illusion of Security

I climbed a ladder last week to dust the ceiling fan.

I finally had time for it. No travel schedule. No meetings. No early flights to catch. Just a regular Tuesday afternoon in my own house, doing the small domestic tasks that pile up when you spend sixty percent of your life in airport terminals and conference rooms.

And as I stepped up the ladder — three, four rungs — a thought moved through the back of my mind.

Watch your step. You have no insurance.

Not a panic. Not a crisis. Just a quiet, constant awareness that has become part of the background noise of my days since being spat out.

I brush my teeth a little longer now, so I don't get a cavity I can't afford to fix. I watch my step getting in and out of the car. When I feel a cold coming on, I treat it with everything I know — because a doctor's visit is a calculation, not a given.

I am in my fifties. I have no health insurance.

And here is the particular cruelty of that sentence: I had coverage the entire time I was employed. The moment the company decided I was excess weight — the moment the math changed — that coverage ended. Not gradually. Not with a transition plan. Immediately.

Five years. Sixty percent of my life on the road, building their processes, improving their systems, delivering their results.

And the day they decided I was no longer needed, I became a man climbing ladders with no net.

That is not an accident of the system.

That is the system working exactly as designed.

— — —

How It Was Built

We covered this in Chapter 4, but it bears repeating here in sharper terms.

Employer-sponsored health insurance in the United States was not the result of corporate generosity. It was not a philosophical commitment to worker well-being. It was a workaround.

In 1942, during World War II, the government froze wages to control wartime inflation. Employers couldn't compete for workers by raising salaries. So they began offering health benefits instead — a loophole the War Labor Board explicitly permitted. In 1954, the tax code made it permanent, allowing employers to deduct health insurance contributions and employees to receive them tax-free.

What began as a wartime accounting maneuver became the foundation of how an entire nation accesses medical care.

And built into that foundation — quietly, structurally, without anyone announcing it as policy — was a mechanism of control.

If your healthcare depends on your employer, you cannot easily leave your employer.

If you cannot easily leave, you accept things you might not otherwise accept.

You stay in roles you've outgrown.

You tolerate management you don't respect.

You swallow salary offers that don't reflect your value.

You don't start the business you've been thinking about for three years.

Not because you lack courage.

Because the cost of leaving includes your family's access to healthcare.

And that cost — for most people, in most circumstances — is too high to pay.

The golden handcuffs aren't made of gold.

They're made of fear.

— — —

The Poisoned Carrot

I have an Australian friend who told me about her country's healthcare system.

In Australia, healthcare is not tied to employment. It is not a benefit you earn by staying at a company. It does not evaporate the moment a corporation decides you're a line item. It exists independently of your employment status, because the country made a decision — decades ago — that access to medical care should not be contingent on whether a private employer chooses to keep you on payroll.

When she described this to me, I felt something specific.

Not just envy. Anger.

Because it clarified something I had always felt but never named so precisely.

Healthcare tied to employment is a poisoned carrot.

It looks like a benefit. It is marketed as a benefit. Your offer letter lists it alongside salary and vacation as something the company is giving you.

But it is not a gift. It is a mechanism.

It keeps you dependent. It raises the cost of your autonomy. It makes the question of whether to stay somewhere — or leave, or take a risk, or build something of your own — more complicated and more frightening than it would otherwise be.

Most Western nations decided this was not how healthcare should work.

The United States decided it was fine.

And the people who benefit most from that decision are not the workers.

— — —

The Math Nobody Wants to Do

Let me tell you what the options look like when you get spat out.

COBRA allows you to continue your former employer's health coverage after termination. The catch: you now pay the full premium — both the portion you contributed and the portion the company covered — plus an administrative fee.

In my case, that number is two thousand dollars a month.

Twenty-four thousand dollars a year.

For the same coverage I had while employed.

For coverage that exists solely because a company I no longer work for happened to have a plan.

Two thousand dollars a month is not a healthcare cost.

It is a punishment for being unemployed.

The marketplace plans — the ACA exchange options — are the other door. And they are not straightforwardly better. Depending on your income in a transition year, subsidies may apply. But those subsidies come with conditions. If you get back on your feet — if you rebuild, if you earn above a certain threshold — you may owe money back. The system is designed for people whose income is stable and predictable, which is precisely what it is not in the year you've been spat out.

So you run the math.

Two thousand a month for COBRA, which you cannot sustain.

Marketplace coverage with clawback risk on the subsidies.

Or no coverage, and the quiet arithmetic of watching every step.

This is the choice the system offers a man in his fifties who did nothing wrong except work for a company that decided his position was expendable.

It is not a healthcare system.

It is a gauntlet.

— — —

The Gamble

Every day without coverage is a gamble.

I know this. I think about it. Not obsessively — I refuse to let it consume the days I am using to build something better. But it is there. A background hum. A small calculation that runs quietly behind every physical decision I make.

Climb the ladder carefully.

Watch the step.

Brush longer.

Don't ignore the chest tightness — but also don't catastrophize it into a four-thousand-dollar emergency room visit for what is probably acid reflux.

This is what it means to be uninsured in your fifties in the United States.

Not dramatic. Not a crisis every day.

Just a permanent low-grade awareness that one bad moment — one fall, one cardiac event, one diagnosis — could erase everything you have built and everything you are trying to build.

Medical debt is the leading cause of personal bankruptcy in the United States.

Not bad investments. Not reckless spending. Not failure.

Getting sick.

In a country with employer-tied healthcare, losing your job doesn't just cost you income. It exposes you to the single greatest financial risk most Americans will ever face.

And the system built it that way.

— — —

The Bigger Gamble

But here is the question underneath the question.

Not: is staying uninsured worth the risk right now?

But: is it worth going back into a system where your healthcare depends on someone else's decision to keep you?

My answer is no.

Not because employment is always wrong. But because I have now lived, concretely and personally, what it means to have your medical security tied to someone else's spreadsheet. I have felt what it costs — not in dollars, but in the quiet background anxiety of a life where one corporate calculation can remove your safety net overnight.

I don't want to build a life on that foundation again.

What I want — what I am working toward — is enough income from my own work to pay for private insurance outright. Not subsidized by an employer. Not contingent on staying in a role. Mine. Paid for by what I build, not by what someone else permits.

There are also insurance cooperatives — groups that pool risk outside the traditional employer-sponsored framework. They are not perfect. They are not always available. But they represent what the system could look like if it were organized around people rather than employment relationships.

The goal is not to be uninsured forever.

The goal is to reach a position where coverage is something I control — not something I lose the moment a company decides its projections were built wrong.

That is the difference between fragility and leverage.

That is the difference between a life organized around someone else's decisions and a life organized around your own.

— — —

The Illusion of Security

Here is what employer-sponsored healthcare actually provided, beneath the language of benefits and compensation packages:

The illusion of security.

Not security itself. Because real security cannot be revoked by a ten-minute meeting. Real security does not end the moment you become inconvenient to someone else's cost model. Real security is not conditional on continued employment at a company that has already demonstrated it will eliminate your role when the math demands it.

What you had was contingent security.

Which is another way of saying: managed dependency.

You were not protected. You were tethered.

And the tether felt like protection right up until the moment it became a reminder of how little control you actually had.

The forty-hour week contained your time.

The retirement promise deferred your sovereignty.

The healthcare system tied your body's safety to your employer's continued approval.

Three mechanisms. One effect.

A workforce too structured, too tired, and too afraid to build anything outside the system.

That is Part II of this book — and now you have seen all of it.

The question that follows is not whether the system was built for you.

It wasn't.

The question is what you build instead.

That is where we go next.

— — —

Honest Reflections

> *Have you ever stayed in a job longer than you should have — or accepted less than you deserved — because leaving would mean losing healthcare coverage? What did that cost you beyond the financial calculation?*
>
> *If healthcare were not tied to employment — if it existed independently of who was paying your salary — what professional decisions would you have made differently? What risks would you have taken?*
>
> *Sit with the real number: what does it cost to be uninsured right now? Not just financially — but in the background anxiety, the modified behavior, the quiet calculations? Are you honest with yourself about what you're carrying?*
>
> *What is your plan for coverage that doesn't depend on an employer? Not the plan you hope to have someday — the actual next step you can take this month.*

> *Is the goal to get back into a system that can revoke your coverage with a ten-minute meeting — or to build a position where coverage is something you control? What would it actually take to get there?*

PART III Stabilize Before You Move

Chapter 7: The Money Clock Is Ticking — Financial Triage for the First 30 Days

Part Two was about understanding the system that produced what happened to you. The forty-hour week designed to contain you. The retirement promise that was always a carrot. The healthcare tether that traded your body's safety for your employer's approval.

Understanding the system is not enough. What comes next is what you do about it — starting now, starting with the most immediate reality in front of you.

The money.

— — —

Give yourself two days.

Not two weeks. Not two months. Two days.

Sleep late. Watch television. Sit on the couch and let the shock do what shock does. You have earned the right to feel it without immediately performing recovery.

But on day three, the clock is running whether you acknowledge it or not.

And the people who do best in the months following a layoff are almost always the ones who sat down early — not in a panic, but with clear eyes and a spreadsheet — and got honest about where they actually stood.

That is what I did on day three.

I opened an Excel file my wife and I had built two months earlier — a holding cost breakdown for our rental property, with a separate tab for our primary home's monthly expenses. I added a few rows: the streaming subscriptions, the weekly staples, the things that don't feel like expenses until you are counting every dollar.

Then I sat down with my wife and went over the numbers.

Not dramatically. Not in crisis mode. Just two people who had prepared for this possibility, now making it concrete.

That conversation — calm, specific, number-driven — was one of the most important things I did in the first week.

Because the money clock doesn't care about your feelings.

It only cares about the math.

— — —

Why Two Days — Not Zero, Not Twenty

There is a temptation to do one of two things immediately after a layoff.

The first is to go numb — to treat the days after as an extension of the shock, to avoid the financial reality because looking at it makes it more real. This is understandable. It is also dangerous. Every day you delay the honest accounting is a day the clock runs without your awareness.

The second is to go into immediate panic mode — to start sending your resume everywhere, to make frantic calls, to treat urgency as a substitute for strategy. This feels productive. It almost never is. Decisions made from panic are almost always worse than decisions made from position. And you cannot make decisions from position until you know what your position actually is.

Two days of honest decompression followed by honest accounting is not indulgence.

It is the most strategic thing you can do in the first week.

Let the shock settle enough that you can think clearly.

Then think clearly.

— — —

The Spreadsheet That Tells the Truth

Before you make a single call, send a single resume, or make a single financial decision — build the number.

Not an estimate. Not a feeling. The actual number.

What does it cost to run your life each month?

Start with the non-negotiables: mortgage or rent, utilities, insurance, car payments, minimum debt obligations, groceries, phone. These are fixed. They run whether you work or not.

Then move to the semi-fixed: the streaming subscriptions, the gym memberships, the weekly habits that feel small individually and add up structurally. These are the first candidates for reduction — not because they are extravagant, but because they are automatic. You signed up once and they have been running in the background ever since.

Then the discretionary: dining out, entertainment, the monthly outing, the small purchases that compose a lifestyle. These do not disappear — but they get deliberate. One planned outing a month instead of whenever the mood strikes. A grocery budget instead of buying whatever looks good.

When I did this exercise, we cancelled Netflix immediately. We looked at our two cars and considered dropping to one insurance policy — but many state laws require all registered vehicles to be fully insured, so that option was closed. We mapped a grocery approach. We planned one real outing per month and protected it.

None of these changes were dramatic.

Together, they extended our runway by weeks.

And runway — the number of months you can sustain your life without new income — is the only number that actually matters in the first thirty days.

Once you know your runway, the anxiety changes shape. It doesn't disappear. But it becomes specific. Manageable. Something you can plan around rather than something that plans around you.

Math rarely lies — unless you make it.

So don't make it. Run it honestly and let it tell you where you stand.

— — —

Where This Philosophy Came From

I spent years telling other managers the same thing I'm telling you now.

In my industry, there is a busy season and a slow season. Every year, like clockwork, the slow season arrives. And every year, managers who hadn't prepared for it found themselves in crisis — scrambling to cut hours, having uncomfortable conversations with staff who had spent their busy-season earnings as fast as they came in, watching morale collapse under the weight of financial stress that was entirely predictable.

I used to pull my managers into a room before the busy season ended.

I'd put everything on a whiteboard. Historical revenues. Cost structures. The point in the calendar where the numbers reliably turned. I'd walk them through the math: here is when it gets tight. Here is what the labor model looks like if we don't get ahead of it. Here is what happens to your team if they don't know this is coming.

Then I'd tell them to pass it down.

Tell your hourly staff now, while there's still money coming in. Tell them to save during the busy season so they can survive the slow one. Don't let them be surprised by something that shows up on the same date every year.

Position is built before you need it. That was always the lesson.

What I didn't fully articulate at the time — but what became the foundation of my first book, The Leverage Code — was that this same principle applies to everything. Not just seasonal cash flow. Not just hourly staff planning their savings.

It applies to careers. To businesses. To financial lives.

The slow season always comes.

For some people it arrives on a schedule, predictable as the calendar. For others it arrives without warning — a meeting on a Tuesday morning, a ten-minute conversation, a blue folder of HR documents.

But it always comes.

And the only question that matters — the one I had been teaching other people to answer for years — is whether you built position before it arrived.

When my slow season came, I had position.

Not perfect position. Not unlimited runway. But enough savings, enough clarity, and enough of a plan that the shock did not become a spiral.

I also had leverage — in two specific directions.

First, leverage going into any future job negotiation if I needed one. A man who has runway doesn't negotiate from desperation. He negotiates from position. He can say no to an offer that doesn't reflect his value, because the math gives him room to wait for the right one.

Second, leverage as a foundation for building something of my own. Consulting. A small operation. Content creation. The options that require not just courage but cushion — because starting something from zero while financially panicked almost always produces bad decisions and worse outcomes.

Position enabled both.

That is why I wrote The Leverage Code. And it is why this chapter — the one about the first thirty days — is not just about cutting Netflix and filing for unemployment.

It is about recognizing that the work you do right now, in the immediate aftermath of being spat out, is the foundation of whatever comes next.

Map the slow season. Know the number. Build the runway.

Then decide what to build on top of it.

— — —

The Severance Reality

Some companies offer severance. Many don't.

Mine didn't.

They cut and moved on. No package, no negotiation, no gesture toward the years invested. That is the reality for a significant portion of laid-off workers — particularly outside the large financial firms and tech companies that have made generous severance part of their public image.

If you are offered severance, here is what most people don't know: it is almost always negotiable.

The first offer is rarely the only offer. Severance is a financial and legal instrument — the company is typically asking you to sign away certain rights, including the right to sue, in exchange for the payment. That creates negotiating room. You have some leverage. The value of your signature on a release agreement depends on your circumstances, your tenure, and the specifics of how your departure was handled.

Before you sign anything, take the time to understand what you're signing away. You don't need an attorney for every situation. But read the document. Understand the scope of what you're releasing.

Consider whether the amount offered reflects the risk they're asking you to absorb.

The company's attorney drafted that agreement to protect the company.

Nobody drafted it to protect you.

Immorality is not illegal. Most corporations know this and operate accordingly. But knowing what you're giving up — and what you might be leaving on the table — is the minimum you owe yourself before you sign.

— — —

Unemployment — The System Nobody Explains

File for unemployment.

I know that feels uncomfortable for some people. It shouldn't. You paid into this system with every paycheck. It exists precisely for this moment. Using it is not weakness — it is math.

But let me tell you what the process is actually like, because nobody prepares you for it.

When I filed in my state, I discovered that the company I thought I worked for was not, technically, the entity registered with the state unemployment system. Large corporations frequently operate through subsidiaries, holding companies, and related entities — each registered differently depending on location and legal structure.

My initial claim was denied. Not because I was ineligible. Because the company name I filed under didn't match the name on file. It took follow-up to get the claim transferred to the correct entity and approved.

If you work for a large company or one with subsidiaries, be prepared for this. Know the exact legal name of your employer — not the brand name, not the name on your business card, but the entity that appears on your W-2. That is the name you file under, however, that name on the W-2 might not even be it. As was in my case. Follow-up, then follow-up again. It is your money, you or your company paid into that fund for this very reason.

A few unemployment systems have been redesigned to look modern. Some present like a financial analytics dashboard — orange action buttons, KPI-style displays, charts, progress wheels, and other visual indicators of where you stand in the process. For someone who spent their career navigating this kind of interface professionally, it is manageable. For someone working part-time, or for whom English is a second language, or who simply has never worked in an environment where dashboards are the default communication tool — it is genuinely disorienting. Many of those orange buttons, when clicked, led not to required actions but to documents already completed. Confirmations dressed up as action or error prompts.

The weekly benefit amount is, frankly, inadequate.

My state pays one of the lowest maximum weekly benefits in the country. At the maximum rate, the payment covers roughly half of a modest monthly budget — before food. For someone who earned just above average wages, the replacement pay rate is even lower.

There are also limits on how many months you can collect for. Some states have generously extended their unemployment compensation period to 22 weeks, while others are around 13 weeks. It will run out — sooner that you think.

I don't say this to discourage you from filing.

File. Every dollar matters when the clock is running.

I say it so you go in with accurate expectations rather than the assumption that the system will catch you fully.

It will catch part of you.

The rest is on you to build.

— — —

The Three Mistakes That Cost People the Most

In years of working in and around corporate environments, I have watched people navigate layoffs well and badly. The financial mistakes that cost the most are rarely dramatic. They are almost always one of three things.

Panic job searching. Sending resumes everywhere, accepting the first interview that calls back, taking a role that gets you off the financial ledge without considering whether it puts you on a better path or simply back into the same system. This feels like action. It is often the most expensive decision of the transition — not in money lost, but in time lost. Two years in the wrong role is two years not building toward the right one.

Broadcasting victimhood. This one is harder to hear, but it needs to be said. Bad-mouthing the company publicly, framing yourself as someone to whom terrible things were done, making your injury the center of every professional conversation — these feel cathartic in the short term and are damaging in the medium term. The professional world is smaller than it appears. People who come out of layoffs with their reputations intact — and often with new opportunities accelerated — are the ones who speak about what happened with composure and forward focus.

The anger is real. The injury is real. Keep it. Use it as fuel.

Just don't make it your pitch.

Nobody wants to hire someone who is still fighting the last war. And frankly — people are tired of victimhood. There is a cultural exhaustion with it right now. Lead with what you are building, not with what was done to you.

Freezing. The quietest and most common mistake. Staying on the couch past day two. Avoiding the spreadsheet because the numbers feel dangerous. Not filing for unemployment because it feels beneath you, or complicated, or "too much to deal with right now". Letting the days blur into weeks while the runway shortens without your awareness. That is real danger.

The money clock doesn't pause while you process.

Move. Even one step. Even just build the spreadsheet with numbers you don't need to research. We all know our car payment, phone plans, insurance, Netflix, Amazon Prime, and our monthly mortgage. Get those in there.

Movement generates clarity. Clarity generates options. Options are leverage.

— — —

The Move Worth Making Twenty Years Earlier

If there is one thing I would tell my younger self — the one who had not yet been spat out, who was building a career and saving faithfully and assuming the system would hold — it is this:

Start building real assets earlier than you think you need to.

Not a 401(k) that moves with a market you don't control. Not a savings account that inflation quietly erodes.

Property. Income-generating real property. It could be a house, or just a piece of land. Go camping on that land, make use of opportunities it may present, or just watch the trees grow, along with its value.

I own rental property now. It is not liquid — I cannot sell it in a week if I need cash. But it generates income. It holds value. And when I map out the worst-case scenario of this transition, one of my real options is to move into the smaller rental unit, cut my living expenses significantly, and rent out my primary home.

That option exists because of a decision made years ago, not because of anything available to me now.

Leverage is built before you need it.

The best time to plant that tree was twenty years ago. The second best time is today.

Whatever your version of a real asset looks like — property, a side business, a skill that generates independent income, a content library that earns while you sleep — start building it now. Not when you feel stable. Not when you feel ready.

Now.

Because the next time the clock starts, you want more runway and leverage than you currently have.

And here is the part most people miss — the part that separates people who merely survive a layoff from people who are genuinely transformed by it:

The slow season will come again.

Even if you land the dream job. Even if you build the business. Even if everything goes right and the next chapter looks nothing like this one.

Markets shift. Industries contract. Businesses have down years. Health events happen. Life does not run in a straight line for anyone, regardless of how well they plan or how hard they work.

The goal is not to survive this slow season and then relax your position.

The goal is to build position as a permanent practice — something you maintain when you are back on your feet, when the income is strong, when the anxiety has quieted and the urgency has faded. Building position should be a necessary habit.

Build your position with intention.

Increase your leverage continuously.

Know where you stand — not just in the hard moments, but always.

Because the people who get spat out and never fully recover are not the ones who lacked talent or effort.

They are the ones who survived the slow season, got comfortable again, and forgot to keep building.

Don't forget.

— — —

The Anxiety Doesn't Disappear — It Changes Shape

My wife is sharper than me about money.

She is frugal in the way that people are frugal when they understand money structurally rather than emotionally. She tracks it. She plans it. She doesn't catastrophize it.

When we sat down with the numbers, she was steady. Not because the numbers were comfortable — they weren't — but because she understood them. And understanding something difficult is less frightening than not understanding it.

The background hum of anxiety did not disappear when I ran the spreadsheet.

But it changed tone and volume.

Vague financial anxiety is the worst kind. It expands to fill whatever space you give it. It wakes you at three in the morning with no specific concern — just a vague hum in the back of your head. It is a known unknown.

Specific financial awareness is manageable. It says: here is the number. Here is the runway. Here is what needs to happen by this date for the math to hold. It gives you something to work with instead of something to drown in.

We could both go get jobs. Probably within two or three months, at salaries that would stabilize everything.

But you only touch the hot stove once.

Your mother told you when you were a toddler to not touch the hot stove. You did it anyways... I know you did. I did. You learned that lesson once and never forgot it.

Being spat out is the hot stove.

You can go back and touch it again — find another company, rebuild your dependence on their payroll and their health plan and their quarterly projections.

Or you can remember the burn.

And build something that doesn't require you to get that close to the flame.

Honest Reflections

> *Do you know your actual monthly number — not an estimate, not a feeling, but the real cost of running your life? If not, what is keeping you from looking at it honestly?*
>
> *How many months of runway do you have right now? Not how many you hope you have — how many do the real numbers show?*
>
> *What is one expense you have been paying automatically that you have not consciously*

chosen to keep since being spat out? What would it actually cost you to cut it?

Have you filed for unemployment? If not — what is the real reason? Pride? Complexity? Not knowing how? Be honest about which barrier it is, and then address that specific one.

What is the real asset you wish you had started building earlier? And what is the smallest first step toward building its equivalent right now — this month, not someday?

Chapter 8: The Legal Reality Nobody Tells You About

— — —

Note: Nothing in this chapter is legal advice. I am not an attorney. What follows is based on personal experience and general observation — not professional counsel. If your situation warrants legal guidance, consult a licensed employment attorney in your jurisdiction.

— — —

My wife asked me three times.

"Call an attorney. At least you will know."

I had my reasons for hesitating. I had a sense of how the situation looked legally. I had been around enough corporate environments to understand how these decisions get made, how they get documented, and how they get defended. I did not go in expecting a lawsuit.

But she kept asking. And eventually I made the calls.

Four attorneys. Two called back. The first took notes and disappeared. The second called me back, walked me through the situation carefully, and said something I have not forgotten:

"It may be immoral. But it is not illegal."

That sentence was worth every minute of the process.

Not because it opened a door. Because it closed one — cleanly, definitively, with professional clarity rather than personal speculation.

And closing that door is exactly what I needed to move forward.

— — —

The Known Unknowns

There is a concept that applies perfectly to the legal question after a layoff.

The known unknowns.

You know that you don't know something. You are aware of the question. You just don't have the answer. And that gap — between the question you can articulate and the answer you don't have — is where anxiety lives.

After being spat out, most people carry a version of this question:

Was what they did to me legal?

They may not be planning to sue. They may not even be particularly angry anymore. But the question sits there, unresolved, in the background — like all unanswered questions — consuming a quiet portion of their mental energy every day.

Getting a legal opinion doesn't necessarily give you a case.

But it gives you an answer.

And an answer — even one that says there is nothing to pursue — is infinitely more useful than a question that never gets asked.

"Now I know" allows you to keep moving forward.

A known unknown breeds anxiety.

An answered question — even an unfavorable one — sets you free.

— — —

Immoral Is Not Illegal — And That Matters

Here is something the corporate system understands very well and most employees do not:

The bar for illegal is much higher than the bar for unfair.

A company can make decisions that feel deeply wrong — that violate every reasonable standard of decency and reciprocity — and still be operating entirely within the law.

They can eliminate your role the week after your best performance review.

They can cut you while keeping someone less experienced and less productive.

They can end a seventeen-year career with a ten-minute meeting and a scripted apology.

All of that can be immoral.

None of it is necessarily illegal.

The law protects specific things. It protects against discrimination based on protected class — race, gender, age, disability, religion, national origin, and others depending on jurisdiction. It protects against retaliation for legally protected activities. It protects against certain procedural violations in how terminations are handled.

What it does not protect against is a corporation making a cold, financially motivated decision that happens to end your career.

In my case, the attorney was direct. I am in a protected class. But the decision was not made based on my protected class — it was part of a broader reduction in which six people were laid off over nine weeks. In that context, the individual termination becomes harder to isolate as discriminatory. The math — the corporate math, the same math we have discussed throughout this book — provides its own defense.

It was a cost decision. They cut costs. You were a cost.

Not illegal.

Not right.

But legal.

Knowing that distinction clearly — and getting a professional to confirm it rather than letting it simmer as a question — is one of the most important things you can do in the first thirty to sixty days.

— — —

What You Probably Signed Without Reading

When you were hired, you signed documents.

Most people do not read them.

Not because they are careless. Because they are excited. Because the job offer is in hand and the paperwork feels like a formality between the offer and the first day. Because the stack is thick and the language is dense and nobody in the onboarding process stops to explain what any of it actually means.

The company's attorneys wrote every word of those documents.

Every clause. Every definition. Every limitation of liability.

They were written to protect the company. Not you.

And among the documents you may have signed — possibly without fully understanding what you were agreeing to — there may have been an arbitration agreement.

An arbitration agreement waives your right to sue the company in court. Instead of a judge and jury, disputes go to a private arbitration process — one that research consistently shows favors employers over employees, partly because arbitration firms depend on corporate clients for repeat business in a way that creates structural bias, and partly because the process is private, which means outcomes are not publicly reported and do not build legal precedent that might protect future employees.

When my company sent out arbitration agreements for employees to sign, I ignored it.

Not dramatically. I simply did not return it.

It never came up again.

That is not a universal experience — some companies follow up, some make signing a condition of continued employment. But it illustrates something worth understanding: these agreements are often treated as routine administrative paperwork when they are, in fact, significant legal instruments that change the landscape of any future dispute.

If you are currently employed, find out whether you have signed an arbitration agreement and what it covers.

If you are being onboarded at a new company, read the arbitration clause before you sign. Ask questions. Understand what you are giving up.

You may still choose to sign — employment sometimes requires it. But sign with awareness, not by default.

— — —

What Your Harassment Training Already Told You

Here is something worth recognizing.

If you worked in management at any point in the last decade, you almost certainly completed harassment and compliance training.

And that training — which most people sat through quickly, clicked through the modules, passed the quiz, and moved on from — actually told you a great deal about your legal rights as an employee.

Because the purpose of that training is not only to protect the company from your behavior.

It is to teach you what illegal workplace conduct looks like — which means you were trained, whether you absorbed it fully or not, to recognize discrimination, retaliation, hostile work environment, and other legally actionable behaviors.

The company trained you what not to do.

Which is also a training in what should not be done to you.

If something happened in the lead-up to your termination that felt wrong in a specific way — not just unfair, but potentially retaliatory or discriminatory — you may already have a framework for recognizing it. You were given that framework by the company itself.

Pay attention to that. If emails exist that document something inappropriate, keep them. If conversations happened that crossed a legal line, write down the dates, the participants, and what was said while the details are still fresh.

You may never need any of it.

But documentation is the foundation of any legal claim, and the window to gather it closes quickly once you are out the door.

— — —

How to Approach the Attorney Conversation

If you decide to consult an employment attorney — and I recommend at least one conversation — here is what to expect and how to make it useful.

Not every attorney will call you back. I contacted four. Two responded. One ghosted me after the initial call. One followed through. That ratio is not unusual, and it is not personal. Employment attorneys receive a high volume of inquiries and prioritize cases they believe have legal merit and financial viability.

Do not let the non-responses stop you from finding the one who engages.

When you do connect, come prepared. Have the timeline clear in your mind: when you were hired, what your role was, when and how the termination happened, who was in the room, what was said, whether others were laid off around the same time, and whether anything in the lead-up felt retaliatory or targeted. Bring a "one pager", a typed up report with a timeline, names, dates, and facts. Not emotions. They are looking for illegalities, not emotions.

The attorney will likely ask about documentation — the termination letter, any performance reviews, any written communications that are relevant. Present what you have.

Then listen to what they tell you.

The goal of this conversation is not to build a case. It may become that — but the primary goal is to get a professional assessment of your situation so that you can move forward with clarity rather than speculation.

If they tell you there is no legal case, that is information.

Valuable information. It closes the known unknown. It lets you redirect your energy away from the legal question and toward the building question.

If they tell you something actionable may exist, that is also information.

But in either case, you will know. And knowing — even when the answer is not what you hoped — is always better than carrying a question that never gets answered.

— — —

What Severance Documents Are Actually Asking You to Sign

If you were offered severance, there was almost certainly a document attached to it.

That document is not a thank-you note.

It is a legal release — a contract in which you agree, in exchange for the severance payment, to give up specific rights. Most commonly, the right to sue the company for claims related to your employment and termination.

This is standard practice. It is also a negotiation, even when it is not presented as one. You have leverage here.

Companies routinely offer the minimum they think you will accept. The first number is not always the final number. And the scope of what you are releasing — whether it covers only federal claims, or state claims as well, or specific categories of potential legal action — is something an attorney can help you understand before you sign.

The clock on these agreements is real. Most give you twenty-one days to review and seven days to revoke after signing. If you are over forty, federal law may entitle you to additional protections under the Older Workers Benefit Protection Act.

Do not sign on the day it is handed to you. It will be tempting, but don't do it.

Take the time you are given.

Read what you are releasing.

And if the severance is significant enough to matter to your runway, spend a few hundred dollars on an attorney to review it before you sign away rights you might not even know you have.

— — —

The Emotional Function of Legal Clarity

I want to close this chapter on something that is not strictly legal — but is deeply connected to why this chapter matters.

My wife thinks in micro. She sees the trees. I think in macro. I see the forest.

When she told me for the third time to call an attorney, I heard something different than a legal strategy.

I heard: stop carrying this question. Get the answer. Then put it down.

That is the emotional function of legal clarity.

Not every layoff warrants a lawsuit. Most don't. The attorney may tell you — as mine told me — that what happened was immoral but not illegal, and that the circumstances don't support a viable claim.

That answer is not a defeat.

It is a release.

It tells you: this chapter is closed. The question has been answered by someone qualified to answer it. You can stop rehearsing the argument in the shower at six in the morning and redirect that mental energy toward the thing that actually matters now.

What you are building next.

The legal reality of your layoff is worth understanding.

But it is not worth getting stuck in.

Get the answer. Then move.

— — —

Do you know whether what happened to you was legal? Not whether it was fair — whether it was legal. If you don't know, what is stopping you from finding out?

Have you signed an arbitration agreement at any point in your career — current employer or past? Do you know what it covers and what rights it asked you to waive?

Is there a known unknown about your termination that is quietly consuming mental energy right now? What would it mean to get that question answered — even if the answer is not what you hope?

If you were offered severance and signed a release, do you know what you gave up? Did you read it before you signed it?

What did your harassment and compliance training actually teach you about your own rights as an employee? Have you ever applied that knowledge to evaluate what happened to you?

Chapter 9: Who Are You Without the Job?

There is a joke my wife and I have told more than once over the years. After the layoff, it made even more sense to me.

A family is trapped on the roof of their house in a flood. The water is rising. The father is calm — certain that God will intervene.

A boat appears. The rescue worker calls up: "Come on — get in."

The father waves them off. "No thank you. God will help us."

A second boat arrives. Same offer. Same answer.

A helicopter drops a rope. The father declines again.

The family is swept away.

When the father reaches the pearly gates, he looks at God with confusion and grief. "Why didn't you save us?"

God looks back at him.

"What do you mean? I sent you two boats and a helicopter."

My wife and I had been telling ourselves for over a year that the signs were there. The physical demands of a job that required sixty percent travel were accumulating in a body that was getting older. The industry was shifting. The appetite for what we actually wanted — remote work, creative freedom, travel for pleasure instead of obligation — had been building for longer than we acknowledged.

The layoff was the helicopter.

We could keep waiting for a different kind of rescue. Or we could grab the rope.

— — —

What the Job Was Actually Giving You

Most people, when they lose a job, think they are grieving the income.

Sometimes that is true. But income is rarely the whole story.

Jobs give people things that have nothing to do with the paycheck. Structure. Purpose. An audience for their skills. A context in which their identity makes sense to the world and to themselves.

For me, it was not the title I missed. It was not the colleagues — I was rarely in one place long enough to build the kind of bonds that ache when they're severed.

What I missed was the coaching.

The moment a new manager finally understood why we had built the systems the way we did — why the preparation mattered, why the process was not bureaucracy but a solid working plan. The look on their face when the team executed and it worked. When game day arrived and everything held because the foundation had been laid correctly.

That instant gratification — seeing preparation become performance — is something I had not separated from the job itself. I thought I missed the job. What I actually missed was teaching, the consulting, and the high that comes with everything falling into place. The job had been the vehicle. The thing I loved were the components under the hood.

That distinction matters enormously.

Because if you think you miss the job, you will go looking for another version of the same job.

But if you understand what the job was actually giving you — the specific function it served in your sense of self — you can start asking a different question.

What did you love doing?

Why did you love it?

Where else can I get that?

How else can I do the thing I actually love — without the parts of the structure I was ready to leave or forced out of?

— — —

The Skills Are Yours

When the role disappears, there is a quiet fear that the skills went with it.

That the expertise you built over decades was somehow attached to the company, the title, the org chart — and that without those containers, the ability itself is diminished.

It is not.

The skills you built belong to you. They always did. The company rented the application of your skills. They did not own your skills.

I am a process and management improvement professional. I spent a career making things work better — identifying inefficiencies, building systems, changing how managers think, and training the people who would run those systems long after I moved on. That capacity did not leave when the badge and laptop were deactivated.

What changed was the context.

And changing the context is not a loss. It is an opportunity to choose a better one.

I can teach people how to reorganize their business. I can help someone write their first book. I can apply a process improvement mind to content creation — making it faster, more systematic, more scalable. The same brain that built operational systems for a global company can build content systems for an independent creator.

The application changes. The capability doesn't.

Whatever your version of this is — the thing you were actually good at underneath the title — that is still yours. The question is not whether you still have it.

The question is where you want to apply it next.

— — —

The Relief You Weren't Supposed to Feel

There is a feeling many people have after a layoff that they do not talk about.

Relief.

Not because the loss isn't real. Not because the financial stress isn't genuine. But because some part of them — the part that had been watching the signs accumulate and choosing not to act on them — recognizes that something necessary has happened.

Sixty percent travel is not a job description. It is a consumption of life.

For years, the airports and hotel rooms and back-to-back support visits were the rhythm. And the rhythm worked — until the body started keeping score in ways that couldn't be ignored. The physical demands of that life compound differently at fifty than they did at thirty-five. The tolerance decreases. The recovery time lengthens. The appetite for it changes.

I had always wanted to consult independently. To travel for leisure instead of obligation. To visit family overseas without calculating it against a quarterly calendar.

The job had been getting easier with time, in terms of competency. But the body was not keeping pace. And something in the arrangement had started to feel like a trade that no longer made sense — not financially, but existentially.

The relief I felt when it ended was not ingratitude.

It was recognition.

The boats had been coming for a while.

I had just been waving them off.

— — —

The Identity That Was Always Underneath

Here is the question this chapter is really asking:

Not who were you when you had the job...

But who were you before it? Who have you always been, underneath the title and the travel schedule and the professional identity the role provided?

I am curious. Deeply, constitutionally curious. I always have been.

During the working years, that curiosity was channeled into the job — into solving operational problems, into learning new markets, into understanding why some management teams thrived and others struggled. The job gave curiosity a container.

Now the container is gone.

And the curiosity has nowhere to go but everywhere.

I am learning about artificial intelligence and how to use it to create faster and better. I am writing books — this one, and others before it. I am building content. I am teaching myself to promote what I build, which is harder than building it, and I am asking questions of anyone and any tool that can help me get better at it.

I am stressed about money. That is true and I am not going to pretend otherwise.

But I am not standing at the edge of a cliff. And more importantly — I am doing work I actually care about, on a schedule I actually control, exploring subjects I am genuinely interested in.

I am free to be curious on my own schedule now.

Not when I can squeeze it between work days, events, and flights.

That freedom is real. It was always available. The job — the structure, the obligation, the identity it provided — was also what blocked access to it.

The layoff removed the block.

That is the helicopter.

— — —

The Daily Texture

Most conversations about reinvention focus on the destination.

The new career. The business. The financial target. The five-year plan.

Those things matter. But they are abstractions until you can describe something more concrete:

What does your day actually look like when you are living the life you want?

Not the income statement. The daily texture.

For me, the answer has become clear in the weeks since the layoff — partly because I am living a version of it now, and partly because living it has clarified what it actually needs to contain.

Two to three hours of focused work in the morning or evening. Writing. Building content. Consulting with a client on a problem I find genuinely interesting. Using the same process improvement mind that organized operational systems to organize creative systems — making the work faster, more repeatable, more scalable.

Enough income to sustain the life and build position toward the future. Not a number that requires sixty-percent travel or seventy-hour weeks. A number that reflects the actual value of the work, earned on terms that make sense.

Time with my wife. Not scheduled around a travel calendar but woven into the rhythm of the week.

Exploring things together — historic places, new countries, the kind of travel that feeds curiosity rather than depletes energy.

Variety. The freedom to be interested in more than one thing, to move between subjects, to teach and learn and create without a single employer defining the scope of what is relevant to my role.

That is not a fantasy. It is a design.

A dream becomes reality when there is a plan behind it.

And the reason I can describe it this clearly is that being spat out forced me to articulate it — to stop deferring the question of what I actually want until some later date that kept moving further away.

Life is not about work.

Work is about funding and filling the life.

For a long time, those two things were inverted.

They are not anymore.

— — —

The Signs Were Already There

You may be reading this in the first days after your own layoff, still in the shock of it.

Or you may be weeks out, past the initial numbness, starting to feel the pull of something you cannot fully name yet.

Either way, I want to ask you something.

Were the signs there before this happened?

Not signs of the layoff specifically – signs of the misalignment. The growing sense that the trade you were making – your time, your energy, your best years – was no longer returning what it once did. The fantasy you kept returning to. The thing you said you would do "someday" that kept getting deferred.

For many people, the layoff is not the arrival of a new problem.

It is the forced resolution of an old one.

The boats were already coming. You were already on the roof. The question was just whether you would wait for a rescue that looked exactly like what you expected – or grab the rope that was actually being lowered.

This is not the end of who you are.

It is the beginning of who you were always going to be once the structure that was holding you in place was finally removed.

The title is gone.

The badge is deactivated. The laptop is inaccessible.

The calendar that used to organize your existence has been decommissioned.

What remains is you.

Find out who that is.

Then build accordingly.

— — —

Honest Reflections

What did the job actually give you that had nothing to do with the paycheck? Structure? Purpose? An audience for your skills? An identity that made sense to other people? Be specific — because what you name here is what you need to find again, in a context you control.

> *What is the thing underneath the title — the capability, the drive, the thing you were actually good at — that belongs to you and not to the company? Where else can you apply it?*
>
> *Were the signs already there? Not of the layoff — of the misalignment. What were you choosing not to act on, and why?*

Describe the daily texture of the life you actually want. Not the income target — the actual day. What time do you start? What do you do? Who are you with? What does it feel like? If you cannot describe it yet, start with the one element you are most certain about.

Who are you right now — not who you are trying to become, but who you actually are today, standing in it? What is still intact? What is still yours? What has this cleared away that needed to go?

Part III is complete.

You have stabilized. You have looked at the money honestly. You have gotten the legal clarity you needed. You have started the identity work of understanding who you are when the role is stripped away.

Now comes the part this whole book has been building toward.

Not surviving what happened.

Building what comes next.

Part IV begins with the most important shift you will make in this entire process — not a financial decision, not a career decision, but a thinking decision.

From employee to strategist.

Let's go.

PART IV Reposition and Reinvent

Chapter 10: From Employee Thinking to Strategic Thinking

There is a phrase that used to make my blood pressure rise.

Every single time.

"We have always done it this way."

I heard it in every organization I ever worked in. From managers who had been doing the same job for fifteen years. From teams that had stopped asking why the process existed and were simply executing it because it had always been executed. From people who had mistaken familiarity for wisdom and routine for strategy.

"We have always done it this way" is the sentence that marks the boundary between employee thinking and strategic thinking.

Not because employees are unintelligent.

But because the system they operate within does not reward the question that should always follow it:

But should we?

— — —

What Employee Thinking Actually Looks Like

Employee thinking is not laziness. Let me be clear about that.

Some of the hardest-working people I have ever encountered were trapped in employee thinking. They showed up early, stayed late, executed faithfully, delivered consistently.

But their thinking was bound.

An employee thinks about the task at hand and what the next person down the line needs. The horizon of their thinking is the next step. The next handoff. The next deliverable.

That is not a character flaw. It is the natural result of operating inside a structure that was built to channel thinking in exactly that direction. The employee's job is to execute within the framework — not to redesign it. The corporate system rewards reliable execution and punishes unsanctioned deviation. Over time, the thinking conforms to the reward structure.

The tells are specific.

"I like to do that on Mondays when it is slower." Translation: I defer the difficult thing to the day I have built a story around being easier. But Monday is not easier. Monday is harder — because you spent the weekend knowing the thing was waiting, and now it sits at the front of a full week instead of the back of a completed one.

"I will do that tomorrow." Tomorrow will be harder than you think. Because you are making it that way. Every deferral compounds the weight of the thing deferred. The employee thinks tomorrow will be lighter. The strategist knows tomorrow carries today's unfinished weight plus its own.

"That is not my job." This one is the most honest version of bounded thinking — and in some contexts, the most self-protective. But it is also the clearest signal that someone has stopped asking what needs to happen and started asking only what they are responsible for.

Employee thinking does many tasks well within a defined lane.

Strategic thinking asks whether the lane is going in the right direction.

— — —

What Strategic Thinking Actually Is

A strategist looks at the entire process.

Not the next step. The whole thing. Start to finish. Resources in, outputs out, friction points in between, and the gaps between what the process assumes and what reality actually delivers.

A strategist rips it apart. Puts it back together. Asks what the original design was optimizing for — and whether that is still the right thing to optimize for given where things stand today.

But the most important thing a strategist does — the thing that most clearly separates strategic thinking from employee thinking — is pivot.

Employees don't pivot. The structure they operate within rarely permits it. Deviation from the established process is a risk, and risk in a corporate environment is usually discouraged unless it is your job to manage it.

Strategists pivot. And the sophistication is not just in knowing when to pivot — it is in knowing how much.

Do I pivot everything, or take a part of the current approach with me? Do I keep going even though I am outside my comfort zone, trusting that the discomfort is the price of progress? Do I rebuild from scratch, or do I modify what already works?

Those questions require a kind of thinking that the employee frame rarely develops — because the employee frame was never designed to need it.

Strategic thinking is also iterative in a specific way.

Try. Learn. Try again. Learn again. Pivot if the data demands it.

Not failure. Not success. A feedback loop.

Employees are trained to execute correctly the first time. Strategists are trained to learn faster than the problem evolves.

— — —

The Moment the Shift Happened for Me

I did not always think like a strategist.

There was a period early in my career when I operated solidly within the employee frame — executing well, delivering reliably, thinking about my lane and the next handoff and not much further.

What changed it was a person.

I worked alongside a woman in sales who thought in a way I had never encountered. Her ideas were out of the box in the truest sense — not incrementally creative, not variations on existing approaches, but genuinely different in their architecture. She saw possibilities where I saw operational obstacles. She proposed things that were, from my execution-focused perspective, amazingly hard to implement.

And she her idea was the right thing to do. Almost every time.

Working with her forced me to change the way I thought. Her ideas were my operational challenges. I could not keep up with her by thinking the way I had always thought. I had to stretch the frame. I had to build and strategize.

What I discovered was that I did not need to match her creative leaps. What I needed was to take her vision and find the version of it that could actually be built. To draw up plans that would work in the real world. To come back to her not with "we can't do that" but with "here is how we could do something like that in a way that actually holds together."

Often she loved the modified version better than the original.

So did I.

We succeeded. Won awards. The business grew.

And I came out of that experience understanding something I had not known going in: strategic thinking is not about having the biggest ideas. It is about being able to look at any situation — especially a difficult or constrained one — and find the path through it that most people cannot see because they stopped looking at the whole picture.

— — —

Pressure Creates Diamonds or Crushes Wood

Being spat out is pressure.

Real, specific, financial and existential pressure. The kind that does not allow you to defer the hard questions to a "Monday" that feels slower.

And pressure does one of two things.

It creates diamonds.

Or it crushes wood.

The difference is not talent. It is not luck. It is not even experience, though experience helps.

The difference is whether the person under pressure reacts or responds. Whether they collapse into the structure they know — frantically rebuilding the employee frame because it is the only frame they have — or whether they use the pressure as the forcing function it actually is.

Strategic thinkers think their way out of bad situations. Not always immediately. Not always painlessly. But they do not stop at the wall. They look for the door, or the window, or they start asking whether the wall actually needs to be there at all.

They also — and this is the part that separates good strategists from merely resilient ones — look for what can be used.

Not just survived. Used.

The layoff is painful. It is also data. It tells you something about the system you were operating in, the value the system was willing to assign to your contribution, and the gap between what you built for them and what you could build for yourself.

A strategist reads that data and asks: what does this tell me about my next move?

An employee waits for someone to assign the next task.

— — —

The Martial Arts of Leverage

Here is the best way I know to describe what strategic thinking built on leverage actually feels like from the inside.

Martial arts.

You may not use it every day. In fact, you may go months or years without a situation that requires it.

But you know what to do in certain situations. You have more confidence than most people in a wider range of circumstances. You know how to react, and how much force to apply, and when restraint is itself a form of strength.

And you have force. Real force. The kind that does not need to be announced because it is simply there — visible in how you carry yourself, in the way you engage, in the absence of desperation in your posture.

Leverage works the same way.

Nobody generally sees your savings account. Nobody knows about the rental properties, or the side income, or the skills that generate value outside your primary employment. They cannot read your runway. They cannot calculate your position.

What they can see is how you carry yourself when a negotiation gets uncomfortable.

Whether you flinch when they push back on your number.

Whether "no thanks" is available to you — or whether the desperation beneath the surface makes it impossible.

Need is desperation. Desperation is weakness. And weakness, in any negotiation, can be used against you by anyone paying attention.

Position is hidden strength. The bank account nobody can see. The option you have not played yet. The "no thanks" that costs you nothing because you have other moves.

Someone who cannot say no is not free. They are constrained — not by law or force, but by the absence of alternatives or options. Every decision they make is made from that constraint, whether they name it or not.

Building position is building the capacity to say no. It is building options.

And "no" — said from genuine strength, without performance or apology — is the most strategic word in the language.

— — —

The Post-It Notes on the Wall

I have large post-it notes stuck to the wall of my home office.

Points I want to make. Things I need to remember. Book titles. Diagrams. Linear plans drawn out so I can see the shape of the thinking rather than just hold it in my head.

Once it is on the wall, my brains is free to expand on it, or add something to my constantly churning brain. This space on my wall frees up space in my brain.

My wife looks at them and sees the points written on the surface.

She does not see the in-between.

The in-between is where the strategy actually lives.

It is dense. It is made of process steps, and alignment questions, and resource requirements, and contingency thinking, and the specific sequence that makes the difference between a plan that looks good on a wall and a plan that actually executes.

This is not a criticism of my wife. She is an exceptional thinker — sharp, structured, strategic within the corporate frameworks she operates in. She sees the trees with remarkable clarity. Having a defined structure frees up her brain to think strategically within it.

What I am describing is a difference in how two people process a problem.

She needs structure first. She builds the framework and works brilliantly within it.

I need the whole picture first. I map the territory before I build the roads.

Neither is wrong. But only one of these modes works when there is no existing structure to operate within.

When you are spat out, the framework disappears. The calendar that beeped at you. The org chart that told you who to report to. The metrics dashboard that told you whether you were succeeding. The entire scaffolding that organized your professional existence.

Gone.

People who crave that structure — who need it, who have organized their cognitive habits around operating within it — will feel the absence like a physical thing. And their first instinct will be to rebuild it. To set calendar reminders for lunch. To create their own chart full of tasks. To build a framework and then work within the framework they just built.

That is not strategic thinking. That is employee thinking applied to a situation that employee thinking cannot solve.

Strategic thinking builds the plan first.

Surveys the whole territory. Looks for opportunities and pitfalls.

Identifies the start point, the end point, the resources required, the pivot points likely to appear, the contingencies worth preparing for.

And then — only then — builds the structure that will support the execution.

Structure is for implementation.

Strategy is for design.

You cannot design your way out of this by implementing harder.

— — —

The Leverage Code as Strategic Operating System

The framework I built in my book, The Leverage Code: Use it to Your Advantage, is not a set of tips.

It is a model for how strategic thinking operates across an entire life — not just in moments of crisis, but as a permanent orientation.

Think about the start, the middle, and the end.

But also think about the many ways to get there — not just the obvious path, not just the path that already exists, but the paths that become visible only when you step back far enough to see the full terrain.

Build position. Build leverage. Build options.

Not as a defensive posture — as a permanent practice. Because the strength of your position determines the quality of every decision you make from it. A person with options makes different choices than a person without them. Better choices. Calmer choices. Choices made from what they actually want rather than what they feel forced to accept. Leverage is a force that can counter a force.

Strategic cutting of expenses. Investing in compounding assets. Finding the second income stream before you need it. Saying no to the opportunity that looks good but takes you further from where you are actually trying to go.

These are not financial decisions.

They are strategic ones.

And making them from a strategic frame — rather than an employee frame that is waiting for someone to approve the plan — is the shift that changes everything downstream.

Honest Reflections

> *When did you last say "we have always done it this way" — or think it, even if you didn't say it out loud? What was the situation, and what question were you refusing to ask?*

> *What is your version of the in-between — the dense territory between the visible points of a plan that most people don't see? Are you mapping it, or are you waiting for someone to hand you a map?*
>
> *Where in your life right now are you operating from need rather than position? What would it take to shift that specific situation — not all of it, just that one — toward position?*
>
> *Pressure is on you right now. Is it creating a diamond or crushing wood? Be honest. And if it's crushing — what is the one strategic move that changes the direction of the pressure?*
>
> *What is your version of "no thanks" — the decision, the offer, the situation you could decline if your position were stronger? What would it take to build that strength? And what is the first step, this week, toward building it?*

— — —

Strategic thinking is not a personality trait you either have or don't.

It is a practice. A set of questions you learn to ask before you act. A way of looking at the whole before you execute the part. It is a practiced habit.

It can be developed. It must be developed — especially now, when the structure that used to do some of that thinking for you has been removed.

The next chapter takes the strategic frame and applies it to one of the most emotionally charged questions of any layoff over forty:

Age.

What rebuilding actually looks like at twenty-five. At forty-five. At sixty.

And why the strategy looks different depending on where you are standing.

Chapter 11: Age and Risk – Rebuilding at 25, 45, or 60

Let's start with the thing nobody says plainly.

Retirement is not uncertain.

It is coming. Whether you want it or not. Whether you are ready for it or not. Whether your savings are sufficient or not.

The human body has a design window. Average life expectancy in the United States is just under eighty years. Two out of three Americans will experience some form of cognitive impairment by around the age of seventy. The brain and body are remarkable instruments – but they are not indefinite ones. They run on genetics, on how well you use them, and on whatever medical advances arrive in time to be useful.

The question is not whether the clock is running.

It is whether you are building something with the time that remains – or waiting for a system to take care of you that has already demonstrated it will not.

That is not meant to be grim. It is meant to be clarifying.

Because the strategy looks different at twenty-five than it does at forty-five. And it looks different at forty-five than it does at sixty. And pretending otherwise — treating a layoff as the same event regardless of where you are in the arc of a working life — is one of the most common and costly mistakes people make in the aftermath of being spat out.

This chapter is about the honest strategy at each stage.

Not the comfortable version. The real one.

— — —

At Twenty-Five: You Have the Asset You Cannot See

If you are in your twenties and you have just been laid off, you are experiencing something genuinely painful.

You are also in possession of two assets that you almost certainly do not recognize as assets:

Time. And a pliable brain.

Not in the vague, motivational-poster sense. In the specific, mathematical sense. Every skill you build right now compounds for forty years. Every dollar invested now has four decades to grow. A savings habit established at twenty-five becomes a position that changes how you negotiate every major decision of your adult life. And your brain — not yet calcified by decades of operating within a single framework — can learn new things faster than it ever will again.

Most twenty-five-year-olds do not recognize either of these things. They feel the urgency of the immediate. The rent is due. The peers who stayed employed are pulling ahead on a scoreboard that feels very real in the moment and becomes largely irrelevant within a decade.

Here is what I would tell a twenty-five-year-old right now:

The surfer life is not a failure.

The person who catches waves in the morning, works just enough hours to cover food and rent and a small apartment, teaches surfing on the side, lives intentionally and frugally with a small group of friends and a few pairs of shorts — that person is not behind. They are building something most corporate employees will spend their entire careers trying to achieve: time sovereignty and low overhead.

If that sounds extreme, the principle underneath it is not. At twenty-five, you have no kids, likely no massive debts yet, and a brain that can absorb and apply new information at a pace a fifty-year-old brain cannot match. You can outwork anyone older than you.

Sixteen hours a day...? No problem.

You just do not yet know what to work on.

So here is the practical version: if you can make a thousand dollars a week, save and invest a thousand dollars a month for three years without fail. Take every training opportunity available. Volunteer for projects that teach you how the business actually works — not just your lane in it, but the whole machine. Learn how corporations are intentionally built to make money, invest it to make more, pay their bills ninety days "late" and invest that float, and keep what remains after expenses. That is not cynicism. That is a curriculum. Use the corporate structure to learn structure — and then carry that knowledge out the door when you leave.

Content creation is a valid side path at twenty-five. But it is a side path. You have health and time in abundance. Use them to build the financial foundation first. The creative work compounds better when it is not carrying the full weight of your survival.

The twenty-five-year-old who does these things — even imperfectly, even inconsistently — will be in a completely different position at forty-five than the one who simply rebuilds the same fragile structure and waits for the next slow season to arrive.

— — —

At Forty-Five: The Pivot Window

Forty-five is where the stakes get real in a specific way.

You are old enough to have built something — experience, expertise, a professional reputation, possibly some assets. But you are young enough that a fifteen or twenty-year runway still exists for building something meaningful.

This is the pivot window. The moment when the question stops being "what job do I get next" and starts being "what kind of working life do I actually want to build for the second half."

The trap at forty-five is the same one that traps people at every age, but it is more expensive here: going straight back into the same structure because the financial obligations feel too real to take the risk.

The mortgage. The college tuition or loan payments in full effect. The lifestyle that requires a certain income. The spouse whose career is established and cannot easily relocate. All of it is real. None of it is an argument against strategy — but all of it is an argument against pretending the strategy is the same as it would be at twenty-five.

At forty-five, the move is not to abandon the income — it is to use the income to fund the transition.

Take the next job if you need it. But do not take it as a destination. Take it as a bridge. Use the stability it provides to build the thing you actually want — on the side, in the mornings, on weekends, in the hours that previously went to time on the couch.

The fifteen years between forty-five and sixty are not too short to build something sustainable. They are exactly the right length — if you start now rather than waiting for the moment that feels safe enough to begin.

That moment never comes.

Begin anyway.

— — —

At Sixty: The Honest Math

Here is what nobody says to someone in their early sixties who has just been laid off two or three years before they expected to retire:

Retirement was always going to happen. The layoff just moved up the timeline.

That is not cruel. It is strategic clarity.

Because the person who spends the next two years panicking about the timeline, scrambling to rebuild a corporate career that a sixty-two-year-old body and a changing market may not fully accommodate, is burning the most finite resource they have — time and energy — on the wrong problem.

The right problem is this: what can I build in the next five to ten years that generates enough income to sustain a life I actually want, without requiring me to operate at a pace my body can no longer maintain?

The answer is almost never another full-time corporate role.

It is almost always some version of the same thing: a side income built around what you already know, structured to be sustainable rather than maximal.

If you spent your career growing businesses, teach others how to do it. Get on a board. Become a mentor through a founders platform or a small business advisory network. SCORE — the nonprofit that pairs experienced business people with entrepreneurs who need guidance — is one example of a structure that already exists and actively needs people with your experience.

If you were a specialist — in operations, logistics, finance, healthcare, technology — put yourself on platforms where that expertise is for hire. Upwork, LinkenIn Services, and similar marketplaces exist precisely for this. The barrier to entry is a profile and a willingness to take the first small project.

If you were a mid-level manager at the same company for thirty years — be honest about what you did that not many other people did. Every role, even one that felt unremarkable, contains specific knowledge that someone else needs. The person starting a restaurant needs someone who has managed labor scheduling, food or inventory cost controls, and vendor relationships. The person launching a small logistics operation needs someone who has built systems for tracking or moving things reliably. Your experience is not too narrow. It is too specific to be commoditized — and specificity, in a consulting context, is exactly what people pay for.

Learn to cook. Genuinely. Not as a hobby — as a cost structure. The restaurant habit at sixty is not sustainable on a reduced income. The person who can feed themselves and their household well on a fraction of the dining-out budget has quietly extended their runway by months every year. Home cooked food is healthier too. Less additives. Less salt.

Find the cruise deals. Travel does not have to end because income is reduced. It has to become strategic. Off-season cruises, repositioning cruises, last-minute packages, visiting family overseas and staying in homes rather than hotels, home exchanges — the life you want can still be lived on a deliberately structured budget.

And build the revenue stream — whatever small version of it you can sustain — before you think you need it. Do it while you have the energy, the pliability, and the drive.

A few hundred dollars a week from crafts, print-on-demand, content creation, consulting, teaching, or food service is not a career. It is a lifeline. It is the difference between a retirement that feels like a soft landing and one that feels like a slow emergency.

Because here is the thing no one wants to say directly to someone in their sixties:

The brain or body may give out before you expect. The timeline you are planning around may be shorter than the plan assumes. Two out of three Americans experience cognitive impairment by around seventy. The average life expectancy is just under eighty. Those numbers are not abstractions — they are a design constraint that smart strategy has to account for.

Build the revenue stream now. While the brain is sharp. While the body cooperates. While the energy to learn something new and implement it is still available.

Not because the future is bleak.

But because the future is finite — and the best use of a finite resource is to be deliberate with it.

— — —

The Fifty-Plus Reality

I am in my fifties.

A few years ago I came across a concept called the Age, Health, and Wealth triangle. When you are young, you have long lines for health and time but a short line for wealth. As you move through your forties, the triangle ideally becomes more equilateral — health still strong, time still substantial, wealth beginning to build. By sixty, the American dream version of the triangle says your wealth line should be the longest, compensating for the health and time lines that have naturally shortened.

I think about this triangle differently now.

I believe your early fifties is not the beginning of the end of your productive life. It is the window for semi-retirement — a deliberate pivot away from the forty-plus hour corporate grind and toward something more intentional. Start the business. Launch the consulting practice. Monetize the experience you have spent decades accumulating. Use your wealth line — whatever you have built — to make more. Use money to make money. Build systems and funnels. Grow a customer base.

The goal is not to stop working. It is to become an expert at making money outside the corporate structure — so that when the body and the market eventually make that structure unavailable, you already know how.

Because here is the thing about age discrimination that people talk around but rarely name directly:

It is real. And it is subtle enough to be deniable.

I felt it in the field. Manager outings, trade shows, being sent to locations to train younger managers how to win. They would all go to lunch at the new hot spots — and I would be left with my salad. Not excluded formally. Just not included naturally. The social gravity of the room had shifted, and I was no longer at the center of it.

What I learned to do was use what age actually gave me that youth could not replicate: the clients and senior managers listened. They were open to ideas from someone who had seen most versions of a problem before. I had not "seen it all" — but I was close. And that proximity to experience is worth something specific in a room full of people still building their instincts.

The market values youth in certain ways. It values experience in others. The strategist at fifty finds the rooms where experience is the asset — and stops trying to compete in the rooms where it is not.

Here is the rest of the honest picture at this stage.

I have nothing to lose right now. That is not desperation — it is a genuine assessment. The worst realistic outcome is that I find a job. I have about fifteen years of productive capacity in front of me. I do not want to spend them the way I spent the last five. So I will push hard to build something on my own terms — not because I have no other option, but because the hot stove taught me something I will not forget this time.

The time horizon at fifty-plus simplifies the strategy rather than limiting it. I cannot put two hundred dollars a month into a compounding account and expect a million dollars in twenty years. That math does not work at this stage. What I can do is invest that same two hundred into promoting what I am building — books, content, a brand — and grow something that returns faster and more directly than a market account managed by people who collect their fees whether I win or lose.

Followers are currency. Email subscribers are an asset. A customer base — real people who have bought something from you, who trust your name, who will buy the next thing — is worth more than almost any financial instrument available to someone starting from where I am starting.

And if the content does not immediately produce income — there is the food background. The ability to generate revenue selling food is not a fallback. It is a legitimate parallel path. A food concession at a regional fair, a catering operation, a hot dog cart in front of the right foot traffic. Everyone eats. The customer is already there. The question is whether I am willing to get in front of them.

That willingness — to do the unglamorous version of the right thing while building toward the preferred version — is itself strategic thinking that employee mode never develops.

Employees wait for the right conditions.

Strategists work with the conditions they have.

— — —

Risk Is Not the Same Thing at Every Age — But Fear Is

Here is where conventional wisdom gets this wrong.

It says that risk tolerance decreases with age. That older workers are more conservative. That the closer you are to retirement, the less you should gamble.

That framing treats all risk as equivalent. It does not distinguish between types.

In my experience, age does not make people uniformly more risk-averse. It makes them selectively more discerning about which risks are worth taking.

At fifty-plus, I am completely done with certain risks. I will not take another role that requires sixty percent travel and delivers the same outcome as the last one. I will not rebuild a dependency on a single employer's quarterly projections. I will not defer what I actually want to do until a future moment that keeps moving further away.

Those risks feel enormous to me now in a way they did not at thirty-five.

But the risk of starting something? Of building in public, of learning a new tool, of putting a book into the world and seeing who it finds? That risk feels completely acceptable. Because the cost of failure is recoverable. I can find a job if I need to. The floor exists.

What changes with age is not risk tolerance. It is risk clarity.

You get better at distinguishing between the risks that threaten what you have built and the risks that might build something new. Between the risks that put you further from where you want to go and the risks that are the price of admission to where you are trying to get.

Fear, however, does not discriminate by age.

Fear looks the same at twenty-five as it does at sixty. It presents the same arguments. It tells the same story about why now is not the right moment, why the conditions are not quite right, why waiting a little longer is the prudent choice.

The answer to fear is not courage in the dramatic sense.

It is position. When you have runway, you have room to try. When you have options, fear loses most of its leverage over you.

Build the position.

Then make the move.

Regardless of the number on your birthday cake.

— — —

Honest Reflections

Where are you in the arc? Be honest about what your realistic productive window looks like — not the version that assumes everything goes perfectly, but the one that accounts for how bodies and minds actually work over time. Does your current strategy reflect that window?

What risks feel completely unacceptable to you now that you would have taken without much thought ten years ago? What does that tell you about where you are and what you are actually protecting?

What risks feel acceptable right now — even easy — that would have terrified an earlier version of you? What does that tell you about what you have built, and what you still have to lose?

If your productive window is fifteen years, what do you want to have built by the end of it? Not the financial target — the actual thing. The work, the life, the daily texture. Is what you are doing right now pointed in that direction?

What is the small revenue stream — the few hundred dollars a week, the consistent thing built around what you already know — that you could

> *start building this month? Not the empire. The first brick.*

— — —

The strategy looks different at every age.

But the principle underneath it is the same at all of them.

Build before you need it. Move while you still can. Do not wait for the conditions to be perfect — because the conditions will never be perfect, and the window is always shorter than it looks from inside it.

The next chapter takes that principle and applies it to the question that follows naturally from everything we have covered:

Why you should not rebuild inside the same system that just demonstrated what it thinks of you.

And what building outside of it actually looks like.

Chapter 12: Don't Chase the Same System That Spat You Out

The pull is real. I want to state that first.

Because the argument for going back — for finding the next company, sending the resume, landing the role, and resuming the steady paycheck — is not a stupid argument. It is an emotionally intelligent one.

The paycheck appeared every two weeks. Clean. Predictable. Large enough to feel like safety.

The medical benefits were simply there. You did not think about them, plan around them, or budget for them. They covered the toothache before it became a crisis. They absorbed the bill before it became a decision.

And the competence — that quiet confidence that comes from knowing you are genuinely good at something — was constantly confirmed. You walked in, you delivered, you were valued. The feedback loop worked.

That is what corporate employment promises. And for stretches of time, it keeps the promise.

The problem is not that the promise was false.

The problem is that the promise was always conditional — and the condition was never in your favor.

— — —

What the System Is Actually Designed to Do

Eleven chapters have been building toward a sentence.

Here it is.

The corporate system is designed as a trap to create and increase profits for a select few shareholders and wealthy people. It does not care about its workers, its suppliers, or anybody outside the top of the pyramid. Shareholders invest to make money. Period.

That is not cynicism. That is the legal and structural reality of how publicly traded corporations operate. The fiduciary duty of a public company runs to its shareholders — not to its employees, not to its communities, not to the people who gave decades of their working lives to its growth.

When you were useful to that system, it kept you. When the spreadsheet said you were a cost that exceeded your contribution to shareholder value, it removed you. Not maliciously. Not personally.

Efficiently.

You were a cost. They cut the cost. That is the system functioning exactly as designed.

Understanding this is not about bitterness. It is about clarity. Because you cannot build a strategy for what comes next if you are still operating under the illusion that the system is something other than what it is.

It is a machine. You were a part. The machine continues without you. Acknowledge it happened and learn from it.

The question is what you build now that the machine no longer defines you.

— — —

Is There a Version That Is Not a Trap?

This is a fair question. And it deserves a direct answer.

Every publicly traded corporation is ultimately a trap of the same design. The shareholders rule. The quarterly earnings call sets the agenda. The employee, however valued, is always subordinate to the number.

But there is a category worth knowing about.

Employee-owned companies — structured as Employee Stock Ownership Plans, or ESOPs — operate differently in measurable ways. The research is consistent: ESOP companies retain employees at roughly three times the rate of publicly traded firms. During the COVID-19 pandemic, when corporations cut headcount sharply, employee-owned companies were over three times more likely to retain their workers. They contribute significantly more to retirement — studies show ESOP participants carry more than double the average retirement savings of comparable workers at non-ESOP firms.

The structure is different because the incentive is different. When employees own a stake in the outcome, the relationship between the company and its workforce is not purely extractive. There is a shared interest in the health of the business that does not exist when ownership is held by distant shareholders whose only metric is the stock price and dividends.

Worker cooperatives take this further — each worker gets a vote, decisions are made democratically, profits are distributed based on participation rather than seniority or equity position. They are less common, harder to scale, but represent a genuinely different model of what a company can be.

If you are going back into employment — strategically, as a bridge — these structures are worth seeking out. They are not a guarantee. But they are a different bet than walking back into a publicly traded company that has already demonstrated what it does when the math turns against you.

Most people do not know to look for them.

Now you do.

— — —

The Bridge Is Not the Cage — If You Know the Difference

Let me be honest about something.

There may come a moment — for me, for you, for anyone reading this — when going back to a traditional job is the right move. Not a surrender. A strategy.

The line between the two is not the job itself. It is the intention behind it.

A bridge job is a tool. You take it to extend the runway. To buy more time for the thing you are actually building. To cover the gap between where you are and where the income from your own work can sustain you. You take it with a clear endpoint in mind — five years, eight years, whatever the number is — and you do not stop building while you are inside it.

The cage is when the job becomes the plan again. When the paycheck resumes and the urgency fades and the side project quietly gets deferred to a Monday that never arrives. When the bridge becomes permanent because the comfort of the structure dissolved the motivation to leave it.

You will know the difference by how you feel getting up in the morning.

The bridge: you are not happy going in, but you understand exactly why you are there and exactly what you are building while you are.

The cage: you have stopped asking.

The bridge has an exit ramp built into it from day one. Sell the big house. Rent it out. Reduce the overhead to the point where the income from your own work can cover the life you actually want to live. Medicare kicks in at sixty-five — one of the few government promises that remains structurally intact

— which removes the healthcare anchor that keeps so many people tethered to employer benefits long past the point of wanting to stay.

Plan for the exit from the day you accept the bridge.

Otherwise the bridge becomes a building you live in.

There is one more thing the bridge can be, if you approach it with the right mindset.

A classroom.

The same advice that applies to a twenty-five-year-old returning to corporate employment applies here. You are inside a machine intentionally designed to make money. It has systems, structures, financial games, and operational patterns that took decades and enormous capital to build. None of that knowledge belongs exclusively to the people at the top of the pyramid. It is available to anyone paying close enough attention.

Learn the business, not just your lane in it. Understand how costs are managed, how decisions get made three levels above you, how the company protects its margins and where it is vulnerable. Volunteer for projects that expose you to parts of the operation you have not seen. Ask the questions a strategist asks, not the ones an employee asks —

because you are not really an employee anymore. You are using their infrastructure.

The mindset shift is everything. The difference between someone back in the cage and someone using the cage as a resource is entirely internal. The job looks the same from the outside. From the inside, one person is waiting for it to end and one person is studying while it lasts.

You already know how to do this. You did it the first time around.

Now you do it with intention.

— — —

The Psychological Part Nobody Warns You About

Everyone warns you about the money.

The savings running down. The expenses that do not pause while the income does. The math of the runway and what happens when it ends.

Nobody warns you about the silence.

When you are building outside the system — writing books, creating content, developing a consulting practice, building the audience that eventually becomes the customer base — there is a period that has no external confirmation. No paycheck arriving to tell you the work was worth something. No manager saying the project landed well. No quarterly review confirming that you are on track.

Just you, the work, and the absence of traction.

Traction is the word that matters here. Not sales, not income, not followers — traction. The first sign that what you are building is finding the people it is meant to find. A single book sale from a stranger. A comment from someone who read something you wrote and felt less alone. A direct message asking if you do consulting.

Those moments are small. They are also everything.

Because you can keep your head down and produce — write, create, post, build — for a sustained period without external confirmation. But there is a limit. The psychological part takes a hit when the silence extends long enough to start asking whether the signal is absent or whether it simply has not arrived yet.

This is the hardest part of building outside the system. Not the financial pressure. The absence of the feedback loop that the corporate structure provided automatically.

Inside the corporation, the feedback was constant. The meeting attended. The deliverable approved. The paycheck deposited. All of it said: you exist, you matter, you are making progress.

Outside it, you have to build your own measures of progress. And you have to hold onto them through the stretch between starting and traction — which is longer than anyone tells you, and harder than you expect, and survivable if you planned for it rather than being surprised by it.

Celebrate the small wins. Not because they are enough — but because acknowledging progress, however incremental, is what sustains the work until the larger wins arrive.

The first sale. The first follower who was not your cousin. The first person who found your work without you sending them a link.

Those are not nothing.

Those are proof of concept.

— — —

What Winning Actually Looks Like

Five years from now, if none of this required going back into a traditional corporate role — what does the day look like?

Not the income statement. The actual day.

The book on a national television program. The company that calls and wants to run a seminar series built around what you wrote. The social media account that crossed two hundred fifty thousand subscribers — not because of a viral moment, but because the content was consistent and specific enough that it found the people who needed it.

The revenue that runs at five times the expenses. Not because the number is large, but because the gap between what comes in and what goes out is wide enough that no single client, no single sale, no single platform can close it overnight.

The ability to send money to the kids without calculating whether you can afford it.

No debt. Not as an austerity measure — as a structural condition of a life that does not owe anyone anything.

Working from home. Two to three hours of focused creative work. The rest of the day belonging to the life rather than the job.

That is winning. And none of it is available inside the same system that decided your salary was a cost worth cutting.

The system will not give you that day.

You have to build it.

Which means you have to stop chasing the version of safety that the system offers — the biweekly paycheck, the benefits that are simply there, the feedback loop telling you that you are valuable — and start building the version of safety that cannot be revoked in a ten-minute meeting.

Real safety is not a salary.

Real safety is a customer base that belongs to you. A skill set that compounds independently of any single employer's quarterly projections. A reputation built in public, under your own name, that travels with you regardless of what any company decides to do with its headcount.

The system that spat you out did you a favor you did not ask for.

It removed the cage.

What you do with the open door is the only question that matters now.

— — —

Honest Reflections

> *What is the emotional argument your brain makes for going back? Name it specifically — the*

paycheck, the benefits, the feedback, the structure, the identity. Name it so you can see it clearly rather than letting it operate on you from beneath the surface.

If you took a bridge job tomorrow, what would make it a bridge rather than a cage? What is the specific endpoint — the revenue level, the timeline, the condition — that would tell you the bridge has served its purpose? Write it down before you take the job, not after.

What is your version of traction — the first small signal that what you are building is finding the people it is meant for? Have you defined it specifically enough to recognize it when it arrives? Or are you waiting for something so large it cannot be missed, when the real proof of concept is quieter?

What is the feedback loop you are building to replace the one the corporate structure provided automatically? How will you know, week to week, that you are making progress?

Describe the winning day specifically. Not the income number — the actual texture of the day five years from now if the work succeeds on your terms. If you cannot describe it clearly, you cannot build toward it deliberately. Start there.

— — —

The system is not going to change.

It was not designed to serve you. It was designed to use you efficiently and release you when the efficiency calculation changes.

That is not a reason for anger. It is a reason for strategy.

The final chapter of Part IV is the most practical one in the book.

Twelve exit lanes. Twelve specific paths out of dependence on a system that has already shown you its terms.

One of them is yours.

Let's find it.

Chapter 13: Exit Lanes — Thirteen Paths to Build What's Next

This chapter is not theory.

It is a map.

Thirteen specific paths out of dependence on a single employer. Each one is real. Each one has worked for people who built it correctly and failed for people who approached it with the wrong expectations. The honest version of each lane includes both.

Before you pick one, understand the framing.

Some of these are income replacement — capable of generating enough to live on if built correctly over time. Some are income supplements — best used to extend your runway while something larger develops. Some take years before they pay off meaningfully. The most common mistake people make is choosing the lane that sounds most appealing rather than the one that fits their actual situation, their actual skills, and the actual amount of time and capital they have to build it.

Do the analysis before you commit. Learn to use the tools available — spreadsheets, AI, basic financial modeling — to run a real return on investment calculation for any path you are seriously considering. You do not need a business school degree to do this. You need honesty, a few numbers, and the willingness to look at them clearly.

You also do not need a fortune to start. In this era, capital is less of a barrier than it has ever been. What you need is technology literacy, self-discipline, and the willingness to try, learn, and adjust.

Pick the lane that fits. Then build.

— — —

Lane 1: Independent Consulting

[Income Replacement — Start Immediately]

This is the one most people with deep professional experience overlook because it feels too obvious.

It should not be overlooked.

If you have spent years making things work better in any industry — operations, logistics, finance, healthcare, hospitality, retail, technology — there are businesses right now paying for exactly that knowledge. Small and mid-sized companies cannot afford a full-time process improvement director. They can afford you for a project, a quarter, a specific problem.

Age is not a liability here. It is the credential. The pattern recognition that comes from having seen twenty versions of the same problem is exactly what a founder three years into their business does not have and cannot fake.

Start with what you know. Price it honestly. Take the first client at a rate that feels slightly low — not to undervalue yourself, but to get the case study. Then raise the rate.

LinkedIn is your storefront. Your resume is your portfolio. Your network is your pipeline. You already have all three.

— — —

Lane 2: Content Creation — Books, Video, Podcasts, Newsletters

[Income Supplement → Replacement — Long Build]

Every person who has worked inside a corporate structure for a decade or more has a book inside them.

Not a memoir. A framework.

The concepts of your role. The improvements you drove and why they mattered. The systems you built and how others can apply them. The lessons that took you fifteen years to learn that someone else could absorb in two hundred pages.

This applies whether you ran a department of three hundred or managed a single function in a single location. The specificity of your experience is not a limitation — it is the niche. The person who spent twenty years managing food costs in regional restaurant groups does not write a general business book. They write the book on food cost management for independent operators. That book finds exactly the people who need it.

Content creation is a long build. The honest timeline for a book to find meaningful traction is twelve to twenty-four months of consistent promotion after publication. YouTube channels and podcasts take longer. Newsletters compound slowly and then quickly.

The psychological challenge is the silence before traction. You will produce before you see returns. That is not failure. That is the nature of the build.

The upside is permanence. A book published today continues to sell in five years. A YouTube video posted this month continues to find viewers next year. Content compounds in a way that consulting hours do not.

This is the lane I am personally betting on. My backup is consulting and platform work. Both lanes reinforce each other — the book builds the consulting credibility, the consulting experience generates the next book.

— — —

Lane 3: Teaching, Coaching, and Online Courses

[Income Supplement — High Leverage if Built Correctly]

Teaching and consulting are related but not identical.

Consulting solves a specific problem for a specific client. Teaching transfers a framework to many people simultaneously. The economics are different. An hour of consulting serves one client. An online course built once can serve thousands.

The catch is marketing. Building the course is the easy part. Getting the right people in front of it is where most teaching businesses stall.

One-on-one coaching pays reasonably well and starts quickly — you can charge meaningful rates from the first client. But it scales poorly because it trades time for money in a direct ratio. The ceiling is your available hours.

The high-leverage version is the online course. Build it once. Refine it based on student feedback. Sell it continuously. This is worth pursuing if you have a specific, teachable framework and the patience to market it consistently.

Teaching also functions as a client pipeline for consulting. The person who takes your course and finds it valuable becomes the person who hires you to implement the framework in their organization. Give first. Ask second.

— — —

Lane 4: Freelance and Contract Work in Your Industry

[Income Bridge — Start Immediately]

This is the fastest lane to income after a layoff.

Contract and freelance work keeps you connected to your industry, maintains and expands your network, and prevents the resume gap that the traditional job market penalizes. It also keeps you in the action — exposed to new problems, new companies, new people — without the commitment of full employment.

The strategic value extends beyond the income. Every contract engagement is a potential consulting client, a potential referral source, a potential collaborator. You are not just earning — you are prospecting.

The risk is that freelance work can quietly become a substitute for building something of your own. The income is comfortable enough to reduce urgency. Watch for that. Freelance is a bridge, not a destination.

— — —

Lane 5: Food Business — Catering, Concessions, Pop-Ups

[Income Supplement — High Skill Requirement]

Let me be direct about this one.

The food business is a hard industry. It involves a highly perishable product that can be genuinely dangerous if not handled and held correctly. Temperature controls, food safety certification, health department licensing, supply chain management — the operational requirements are real and non-negotiable.

That said, for someone with a genuine food background — not a hobby, but years of professional experience in food service — this lane has real advantages. The customer is always there. Everyone eats. A well-positioned food concession at regional fairs and events generates cash flow from day one, with low overhead and no lease.

The path in: start small. A single concession, a pop-up, a catering operation built around a specific niche. Learn the local event circuit. Build relationships with event organizers. Scale only after you understand the unit economics of your specific product.

This is a backup lane for people who know food. It is not a hobby lane for people who like to cook.

— — —

Lane 6: Real Estate — Rental Income and Property Management

[Income Supplement — Capital Required]

Real estate is real — the income is genuine, the asset appreciates, and rental income is one of the few cash flows that does not require you to show up and perform every day.

It is also capital-intensive, market-dependent, and full of friction that people underestimate before they are inside it.

If you already own rental property, the strategy is to protect and optimize what you have — not to acquire aggressively in an uncertain income period. If you do not own any, this is a medium-term play, not an immediate one.

The real estate agent path — getting licensed, hanging your license with a broker, working transactions — is a different bet. The industry is dense with part-time agents, and brokers in most states control significant elements of how you operate. The income is commission-based, which means irregular, and the ramp to consistent earnings typically takes one to two years. Research the broker structure in your specific state before committing — the terms vary significantly and matter enormously to your actual take-home.

Real estate rewards patience and capital. If you have both, it belongs in your portfolio. If you have neither, start somewhere else and build toward it.

— — —

Lane 7: Print-on-Demand and E-Commerce

[Income Supplement — Low Barrier, Long Build]

The barrier to entry here is genuinely low. Platforms like Printful, Printify, and Redbubble allow you to design products — clothing, accessories, home goods — and sell them without holding inventory. The platform prints and ships when a customer orders.

The learning curve is real but manageable. Setting up the platforms, understanding the settings, connecting the storefronts — this takes time and patience but not technical expertise. If you have any creative inclination at all, it is learnable.

The hard part, as with all content-based income, is marketing. The product sitting in a digital storefront with no traffic generates nothing. You need an audience, a social media presence, or paid advertising to drive customers to it.

I would look into Shopify and Etsy as a sales and marketing platform. You can quickly connect them with Printify and the other Print On Demand (POD) platforms. Many of the "online shops" have marketing elements built it. Again, you will discover that finding customers is one of the hardest things to do in life and online. Anything you can do helps.

The strategic angle: build the product line around a specific niche — your professional background, your lived experience, your sense of humor about the industries you know. The generic print-on-demand store competes with thousands of identical generic stores. The specific store — built around a point of view — finds its people.

This is a supplement lane. Treat it as a side income that compounds slowly, not a primary replacement.

— — —

Lane 8: Board Positions and Advisory Roles

[Income Supplement — Relationship Dependent]

These exist. They pay. And they are far more accessible than most people assume — if you approach them correctly.

The mistake people make is treating board membership as a destination to pursue directly. It is not. It is a relationship that develops over time when you have demonstrated value to the people who make those decisions.

The path in is :giving first and asking second".

Find a nonprofit whose mission you care about. Find a startup in a space where your experience is genuinely useful. Offer your time. Offer your expertise. Show up without an agenda. Let them see how you think and how you operate when nothing is required of you.

Board seats at nonprofits are more accessible than corporate boards and serve as the credential for larger opportunities. A small startup board is a real board — with real governance responsibilities, real strategic input, and real relationships with founders who will build other companies and remember who helped them when they were small.

Give first. Ask second. The seat comes to the person who made themselves indispensable before they ever asked for it.

— — —

Lane 9: Franchise Ownership

[Proceed with Extreme Caution]

I will be direct.

Franchise ownership requires substantial startup capital — often six figures — plus at minimum six months of operating capital that you do not need for bills or anything else. It will consume your days entirely. The hours are real and they are long.

And here is the question worth sitting with before you sign anything:

If the franchise model were as profitable and straightforward as the sales pitch suggests, why is the franchisor selling licenses to others rather than simply opening more locations themselves?

That is not a rhetorical question. It is due diligence.

If you have the capital that franchise ownership requires, you likely have enough to start something original — without the royalty fees, the brand restrictions, the supply chain requirements, and the contractual obligations that come with a franchise agreement.

If you are seriously interested in a specific franchise concept, work inside a similar business first. Learn the operational reality before you buy the rights to it. Fall in love with the daily work, not the sales presentation. Because the daily work is what you will be doing for the next fifteen years.

— — —

Lane 10: Starting a Small Service Business

[Income Replacement — High Complexity]

A service business is one of the most honest paths to self-employment. You sell a skill or a service directly to clients. There may be no inventory, no product development, no complex supply chain.

The complexity is in everything else.

Finding customers is expensive and competitive. Service businesses in most categories face downward price pressure from competitors willing to work for less. Without an existing community, a strong referral network, or a very specific niche, the early months of client acquisition are a grind.

The operational requirements accumulate quickly: business registration, insurance, accounting, payroll if you hire, permitting depending on the service, fleet management if the work is mobile. You become the jack of all trades whether you planned to or not.

The path to success in a service business runs through specificity. The general cleaning company competes with every other cleaning company. The cleaning company that specializes in post-construction cleanup for a specific type of contractor has a niche, a referral network, and a price point that the generalists cannot easily undercut.

Know your niche. Know your numbers. Know what it will actually cost to acquire a customer before you commit to the model.

Lane 11: Platforms — LinkedIn Services, LinkedIn Profinder, Upwork, and Others

[Income Bridge — Start Immediately]

These platforms exist to connect skilled professionals with people who need their skills. For someone with genuine expertise, they are one of the fastest paths to paid work after a layoff.

LinkedIn ProFinder and LinkedIn Services allow you to advertise specific offerings directly to a professional network that already knows your background. The trust transfer is significant — clients can see your work history, your endorsements, your content, before they ever contact you.

Upwork is broader and more competitive. The honest reality of Upwork for someone with deep professional experience is that your target client is not the budget buyer. It is the business owner who needs a specific problem solved and is willing to pay for the right person. Position accordingly. Do not compete on price with people in lower-cost markets. Compete on specificity and credibility.

Fiverr operates at a lower price point by design and attracts significant international competition. For commodity services, the underbidding is aggressive. For highly specific, experience-dependent work, it is less relevant — but so is the audience. Approach Fiverr with clear eyes about what it is and what it is not.

These platforms are bridges and supplements, not destinations. Use them to generate income and relationships while building something that does not depend on a platform's algorithm or terms of service.

— — —

Lane 12: Building a Personal Brand That Monetizes Multiple Ways

[Income Replacement — Long Build, Highest Upside]

This is the interconnected version of just about every other lane on this list.

A personal brand built around a specific point of view and a specific expertise creates a platform from which multiple income streams operate simultaneously. The book builds the consulting credibility. The consulting experience generates the content. The content builds the audience. The audience buys the course. The course produces the next client. Each element points to the others and supports the others.

This is the highest-upside lane on the list. It is also the longest build and the one most dependent on marketing — which is the hardest skill for most people who spent their careers inside organizations where marketing was someone else's department.

The noise is real. There is more content being produced every day than any audience can consume. Breaking through requires consistency, specificity, and patience that most people underestimate before they start.

But the upside is also real. An audience of two hundred fifty thousand subscribers who trust your perspective and regularly buy what you recommend is not a fantasy. It is a business. It is a business that belongs entirely to you, that travels with your name rather than a company's, and that cannot be eliminated in a ten-minute meeting.

Build the brand. Connect the lanes. Market relentlessly and learn to get better at it. The return compounds in a way that nothing on the traditional employment side of the ledger can match.

— — —

Lane 13: Starting a Small-Scale Marketing Firm

[Income Replacement — High Demand, Learnable]

This one belongs on the list because it is missing from most conversations about reinvention after fifty — and it should not be.

The demand for marketing help among small and mid-sized businesses is enormous and largely unmet. Most small business owners are excellent at their craft and genuinely poor at marketing it. They need someone who knows business and can build a content strategy, manage social media with consistency, run email campaigns, create with Ai, and help them think clearly about who their customer is and how to reach them. Maturity and experience are invaluable in this field.

That is a learnable skill set. It is not a credential that requires years of school. It requires curiosity, the willingness to learn the platforms, and the ability to apply strategic thinking — which, if you have spent a career in process improvement or operations or management, you already have in abundance.

The model: start with one or two small business clients at a modest retainer. Deliver results. Let the results generate referrals. Build the client base incrementally rather than trying to launch a full agency immediately.

The honest challenge: you will need to learn marketing yourself before you can sell it to others. That is not a disqualifier — it is a sequencing note. Learn it on your own projects first. Apply it to your own books and content. Then sell what you have already proven you can do.

The strategic fit for someone rebuilding at fifty-plus: low startup cost, high demand, relationship-driven, and directly complementary to consulting, content creation, and personal brand building. Every lane on this list needs marketing. The person who knows how to do it becomes indispensable to everyone building in every other lane.

— — —

Thirteen lanes. Not one of them is guaranteed. All of them are real.

The one that works for you is the intersection of three things: what you are genuinely good at, what the market will actually pay for, and what you can sustain long enough to build traction.

Do not pick the lane that sounds most appealing.

Pick the one that fits.

Then build it like you mean it.

Honest Reflections

> *Which two or three lanes on this list align most directly with skills you already have and have been paid for? Not skills you want to develop —*

skills you can demonstrate right now to a potential client or employer.

Which lane is your primary bet — the one you are building toward as income replacement? Which is your bridge — the one that generates income while the primary lane develops traction?

What is your honest marketing plan? Not a vague intention to "get on social media" — a specific, weekly action. What will you post, where, how often, and how will you measure whether it is working?

Who in your existing network — former colleagues, clients, managers, vendors — could become your first consulting client, your first course student, your first referral source? Have you contacted them since the layoff? If not, why not?

What would traction look like in ninety days for the lane you have chosen? Define it specifically enough that you will recognize it when it arrives. One client. One sale. One subscriber who found you without being sent a link. Name the signal.

— — —

Part IV is complete.

You have made the shift from employee thinking to strategic thinking. You have looked honestly at age and risk and what rebuilding actually requires at this stage of life. You have understood why chasing the same system is a trap. And you now have a map of thirteen specific paths forward.

Part V is the final section of this book.

It is not about surviving what happened.

It is about building something so solid that what happened can never happen to you in the same way again.

The best revenge is not anger.

It is a life built entirely on your own terms.

Let's finish strong.

PART V Build So You're Never Cornered Again

Chapter 14: Build the Position

You have the map now. Thirteen lanes out of dependence on a single employer. Paths built on what you know, what the market will pay for, and what you can sustain long enough to reach traction.

But a map without ground beneath your feet is just paper.

This chapter is about building the ground. The permanent foundation that makes whichever lane you choose survivable — that gives you enough space from the cliff's edge to make decisions from choice rather than desperation.

— — —

Let's define what we are building away from.

Cornered means you cannot say "no thanks."

It means one crisis feels like doom. It means you do not have options. You do not have leverage. What you have is uncertainty and dread — the specific, exhausting kind that comes from standing too close to the edge. You are on edge waiting for the sword to drop. Every conversation with a potential employer feels desperate because it is. Every bill that arrives carries more weight than the number on it because the number represents something your current position cannot comfortably absorb.

That is what cornered actually feels like from the inside. Not a strategic metaphor. A physical state. The background hum of anxiety that never fully quiets. The decisions are made from fear rather than from choice. The inability to walk away from a bad offer because walking away requires options you have not yet built.

Everything in this chapter — and in this entire book — is about building the permanent distance between where you stand and that edge.

Not because crisis will never come again.

But because the next time it does, you will be standing far enough back that it is a problem to solve rather than a cliff to fall from.

— — —

Position Is Not a Destination — It Is a Practice

The mistake most people make is treating leverage as something you build in response to a crisis — the thing you wish you had assembled before the slow season arrived, before the ten-minute meeting happened, before the paycheck stopped. They think about it reactively, which means they are always building it too late.

The people who are never cornered build it continuously. Not because they are paranoid. Not because they expect disaster. But because the habit of building position is its own reward — and once you understand how the spiral works, you will not want to stop.

— — —

The Spiral

Here is what building position actually feels like from the inside, once it starts to move.

You take one action. Something small — a spreadsheet that maps your actual expenses, a LinkedIn post that puts your thinking in public, a single consulting call with someone who used to be a colleague. The action itself is modest. But it creates something.

Space.

Not physical space. Psychological space. The distance between where you are standing and the edge of the cliff gets measurably wider. The stress that was vague and ambient — the kind that expands to fill every quiet moment — starts to take a specific shape. And specific is manageable in a way that vague never is.

You take another action. The space widens a little more. The confidence that was shaken by the layoff starts to rebuild — not because someone told you that you were valuable, but because you demonstrated it to yourself. You built something. It worked at the small scale. Which means it can work at a larger scale.

This is the upward spiral. Each action creates space. Space creates confidence. Confidence creates the next action. The next action creates more space.

It is a positive, self-fulfilling spiral. And once it starts moving — once you can feel it rather than just understand it intellectually — it becomes something close to addicting. Not in a destructive sense. In the sense that you will not want to stop, because stopping means the spiral reverses and the space closes back in.

Building position is not a chore you do to protect yourself from the future.

It is the most energizing work you will ever do — because for the first time, you are building something that belongs entirely to you.

— — —

What Position Actually Looks Like

Position is not one thing. It is a stack.

Financial position: the runway. The savings that give you time to think rather than react. The assets that generate income independent of whether you show up to a job. The reduced overhead that turns a modest income into a sufficient one. You do not need to be wealthy to have financial position. You need enough buffer between your current moment and the cliff that your decisions are made from choice rather than desperation.

Professional position: the reputation, the network, the demonstrated expertise that means opportunity finds you rather than the other way around. The book with your name on it. The LinkedIn profile that reflects what you actually know. The former colleagues who think of you when a consulting need arises. Professional position is built in public, over time, by consistently showing up and delivering.

Skill position: the capabilities that belong to you and travel with you regardless of which employer holds your contract. The ability to solve a specific class of problems that people will pay to have solved. The new skills being added now — content creation, AI tools, marketing, financial modeling — that expand the range of what you can offer.

Confidence position: this one is underrated and rarely named. The internal certainty that comes from having built things, survived hard moments, and demonstrated to yourself that you can figure out what comes next. Confidence built on evidence is different from confidence built on reassurance. It does not require external confirmation. It does not collapse when someone fails to validate it. It is earned, and it compounds.

You are building all four simultaneously. Each reinforces the others. The financial buffer reduces the urgency that otherwise undermines good decisions. The professional reputation generates the opportunities that build the skill. The skill builds the confidence that sustains the work when traction is slow.

Stack it deliberately. Not all at once — that is how people get overwhelmed and stop. One layer at a time, consistently, until the stack is tall enough that no single event can knock it over.

— — —

The Habits That Build It

Position is not built in dramatic gestures. It is built in small, consistent actions that most people skip because they do not feel enough urgency.

They are never urgent. They are just important.

The financial habit: know your number every week. Not obsessively — once a week, ten minutes, the same spreadsheet. Income in, expenses out, runway remaining, trend direction. This is not anxiety management. It is strategic awareness. You cannot build position you are not measuring.

The professional habit: show up in public consistently. One piece of content per week — a LinkedIn post, a short article, a comment that demonstrates how you think. Not to go viral. To exist in the feed of people who might eventually need what you offer. Visibility is a form of position. The person who has been consistently present in their professional community for two years is not starting from zero when they need a client or a referral.

The skill habit: learn one new thing per month that compounds. Not a certification that pads a resume. A capability that directly serves what you are building. Marketing. AI tools and creation. Financial modeling. Video production. Each new skill is a new lane available to you — a new way to generate value, a new reason for someone to hire you or buy from you.

The income habit: always be building at least one income stream that does not require you to clock in somewhere. It does not need to be large. It needs to exist and grow. The consulting client you take on while employed. The book that sells while you sleep. The course that runs while you travel. Small and growing beats large and singular every time, because large and singular is exactly what got you here.

The network habit: give before you need. Stay in contact with former colleagues, clients, and collaborators during the good periods — not just when you need something. The network that sustains you in a slow season is the one you maintained during the seasons that did not require it.

— — —

The Space Between You and the Cliff

Before the layoff, most people do not know how close they are to the edge.

The paycheck arrives, the bills are covered, and the distance between current stability and financial crisis feels abstract — a problem for some other version of life, not this one.

Then the paycheck stops. And the edge is suddenly visible.

Building position is the permanent practice of keeping yourself far enough from that edge that the view from where you stand is never the cliff. It is the horizon.

The further you build from the edge, the more clearly you can see. The decisions made from safety are better decisions. The negotiations conducted from a solid position are better negotiations. The creative work produced without the background hum of financial anxiety is better work.

Never cornered means never again in a place where "no thanks" is unavailable to you. Where one bad month does not cascade into catastrophe. Where you can look at an opportunity clearly and decide whether it serves you — not whether you can afford to turn it down.

That is what you are building toward.

Not wealth for its own sake. Not security as a comfort blanket.

The permanent ability to say no. Having options is power.

Build it before you need it. Build it while you do not need it. Build it as a permanent practice rather than a crisis response.

And when the next slow season arrives — because it will, in some form, for everyone — you will not be scrambling to build what you should have already built.

You will be standing on it.

— — —

The First 90 Days: What Building Actually Looks Like

Position is a permanent practice. But it starts in a specific moment — and that moment is now, regardless of how many days have passed since the layoff.

Here is what the first ninety days of building position looks like in concrete terms. Not aspirational. Actionable.

Days 1 through 30 — Map the terrain.

Open a spreadsheet. This is non-negotiable. Map every dollar going out and every dollar coming in. Calculate your runway — the number of months you can sustain current expenses before the math forces a decision. This number is the most important number in your life right now. Know it precisely.

Cut everything that is not essential. Not dramatically — strategically. Streaming services, memberships, dining habits, the expenses that accumulated during the employed years when each individual cost seemed too small to matter. Individually they were small. Together they are weeks of runway.

File for unemployment if you have not. Do it this week. The system will not be fast and it will not be generous. File anyway. Every dollar that comes in extends the period during which you can build rather than panic.

Make one professional contact per day. Not a job application — a genuine connection. A former colleague, a former client, someone whose work you respect. Not to ask for anything. To stay warm. To exist in the professional ecosystem while you figure out what comes next. The network that sustains you in month six is the one you maintained in month one.

Days 31 through 60 — Choose your lane and take the first step.

By day thirty you have the financial picture clearly. You know your runway. You know which expenses can be reduced further if needed. You know the approximate timeline before a bridge job becomes necessary.

Now pick the primary lane from Chapter 13. Not the one that sounds most impressive. The one that aligns most directly with skills you already have and can demonstrate immediately. Consulting, freelance work, and platform-based services start fastest. Content creation, personal brand, and online courses build slower but compound longer.

Take the first concrete step this week. Not the perfect step. The first one. A LinkedIn post that puts your expertise in public. A message to a former client offering a specific service. A book outline written down. An Upwork profile created and filled out completely.

The first step matters disproportionately — not because it generates income, but because it starts the spiral. One action creates space. Space creates confidence. Confidence creates the next action.

Days 61 through 90 — Build the habit, measure the progress.

By day sixty, the initial shock has fully metabolized. The daily rhythm of the employed life is no longer the reference point. You are building a new rhythm — one that belongs to you.

Establish the daily and weekly habits that will sustain the build over months and years, not just weeks. The two to three hours of focused creative or productive work. The weekly financial check-in. The consistent professional visibility. The income stream being actively developed.

Measure what matters. Not vanity metrics — real ones. Runway remaining and whether it is holding or shrinking. Professional contacts made and conversations started. Income from independent sources, even if small. Skills being actively developed.

At ninety days, the person who has been building looks materially different from the person who has been waiting. Not necessarily in income — traction takes longer than ninety days in most lanes. But in position. In the thickness of the foundation. In the distance between where they stand and the edge of the cliff.

Ninety days of deliberate action is the difference between someone who survived a layoff and someone who used it.

Honest Reflections

> *What does cornered feel like for you specifically — not the definition, your experience of it? Name the exact sensation, the exact thought pattern, the exact decisions it forces you into. Naming it*

clearly is the first step to building permanently away from it.

What does your position stack look like right now, honestly? Rate each layer — financial, professional, skill, confidence — on a scale of one to ten. Where is the weakest layer? What is the single action this week that starts strengthening it?

What is the one financial habit you are not currently doing that would most directly increase your runway? Not a dramatic change — a consistent small one. What is stopping you from starting it this week?

Where are you showing up in public professionally? If the answer is nowhere, what is the first piece of content — one post, one article, one comment — you could put into the world this week? Not perfect. Present.

Have you felt the spiral yet — the moment when one small action created space, and the space created the confidence for the next action? If yes, what triggered it? If not, what is the smallest possible action that could start it moving?

Chapter 15: The Long Game

There is a difference between making money and building something.

Making money is a transaction. You exchange time, skill, or product for payment. The payment is real and necessary. But when the transaction ends, the ledger resets. The next payment requires the next transaction.

Building something is different. It compounds. Each piece you add makes the next piece more valuable. The audience you grew last year makes this year's book more likely to sell. The reputation you built through a decade of showing up makes the next consulting engagement easier to land. The rental property purchased a decade ago funds the creative work being done today.

The long game is the deliberate choice to build rather than just earn.

It requires a different relationship with time — one that most corporate employment actively discourages, because the quarterly calendar is the enemy of the decade-long arc.

But you are not on the quarterly calendar anymore.

You are on your own timeline now.

Use it.

— — —

What You Are Actually Building Toward

The financial version of the long game is retirement that works.

Not retirement as the system promised it — a defined benefit waiting at the end of forty years of loyalty that turned out to be a 401(k) at the mercy of markets you do not control. But retirement as a structure you build deliberately: multiple income streams, owned assets, reduced overhead, and the skills to generate value in whatever form the market will pay for at whatever age you are when you need it.

The honest reality for anyone in their forties or fifties is that the traditional retirement math is tight. The time horizon for compounding is shorter. The gap between what was saved inside a corporate structure and what is actually needed for a stable retirement is real for most people in this situation.

The answer is not to panic. The answer is to build income streams that do not have a mandatory retirement age.

A consulting practice does not force you to stop at sixty-five. A book continues to sell at seventy. A personal brand built around genuine expertise does not expire when Medicare kicks in. The skills you develop now — writing, teaching, marketing, building — are skills that generate value for as long as the mind is sharp enough to apply them.

This is the long game version of your father's advice: only business owners get rich. Build the thing you own. Let it earn while you sleep, while you travel, while you spend time with the people who matter. That is not a fantasy. It is a structure — and structures can be built.

— — —

Legacy Is Not a Monument

Most people think of legacy as something grand. A building with your name on it. A foundation. A body of work so significant it is studied after you are gone.

That version of legacy is available to very few people and relevant to almost none of the decisions made in the aftermath of a layoff.

The version that matters is smaller and more real.

It is the manager who came up under you — the one who struggled with the system you built together, who finally understood why the preparation mattered, whose face changed when it clicked. That person is running a tighter operation because of the time you spent with them. Their team is better managed. Their customers are better served. That ripple does not stop when you leave the company.

It is the book that finds the person in the first week after their layoff who has no idea what to do next. The one that lands in their hands at the right moment and says: you are not alone, this is not the end, here is what to do.

It is the money sent to your kids without having to calculate whether you can afford it. The trip taken with your spouse or partner that was not earned as a reward for surviving another quarter but simply lived because life is for living.

It is the knowledge passed to anyone who will receive it — through content, through teaching, through the consulting engagement where you give someone the framework that took you twenty years to build and watch them apply it in twenty minutes.

Legacy is not a monument. It is the sum of the useful things you put into the world and the people whose lives were better for having encountered your work.

You are building it right now.

Every chapter of this book is part of it.

Every book you write after this one is part of it.

Every person who reads something you created and feels less alone, more capable, more prepared — that is the legacy. It does not require a corner office or a title or a company that kept you long enough to attend your retirement party.

It just requires the work. Step by step.

— — —

The Difference Between Hustling and Building

The hustle culture version of reinvention says: work harder, move faster, grind longer, outperform everyone around you, and eventually the volume of effort will produce the outcome you want.

There is some truth in it. Effort matters. Consistency matters. The person who shows up and produces when it is hard is further along than the person who waits for motivation.

But hustle without architecture is exhausting and ultimately unsustainable. The person who is simply working harder inside a structure that has no compounding mechanism is just running faster on the same treadmill.

"The harder you work, the more you make" is just not a realistic part of corporate culture.

Building is different from hustling in one critical way:

Building creates things that continue to work when you stop.

The book sells while you sleep. The course runs while you travel. The rental income arrives while you are sitting on a beach somewhere with your friends watching the sun go down over an ocean you have never seen before.

That is not passive income in the lottery-ticket sense as the internet sells it. That is the result of deliberate construction — of building systems that generate value independent of your immediate presence.

The long game is building those systems. One at a time. Each one small at first, and then larger. Each one compounding on the one before it.

Two to three hours of focused work in the morning. The rest of the day for living.

That is not a retirement fantasy. That is the architecture of a life built intentionally rather than defaulted into.

It is achievable.

It requires the long game.

And the long game starts today — not when the conditions are better, not when the income is more stable, not when the fear has fully subsided.

Today. With the next few minutes. One step at a time.

— — —

What You Are Leaving Behind

The long game is also about what you are choosing not to carry forward.

The resentment. The replaying of the conversation that did not go the way it should have. The mental energy spent rehearsing arguments to an audience that will never hear them.

None of that builds anything.

It is weight. And weight slows the upward spiral.

The best revenge is not anger directed at the system that spat you out. It is the life you build in the space the system created by removing you from it. The best revenge is your success.

The day your book is on a national television program. The morning you send money to your kids without checking the balance first. The trip you take because you want to, not because you earned enough vacation days.

That is the answer to everything the system did.

Not a grievance. A life.

The long game requires putting down the weight of what happened and picking up the work of what comes next.

You have already started.

Keep going.

— — —

The Long Game at Thirty vs. the Long Game at Fifty

The principles of the long game are the same at every age. Build things that compound. Own what you create. Generate income from multiple sources. Reduce dependence on any single employer or platform.

But the timeline looks different depending on where you are standing when you start.

At thirty, the long game is about patience and consistency over decades. The compounding account opened now has thirty-five years to grow. The skill developed this year becomes expertise in ten years. The audience built slowly and deliberately becomes the platform that generates income at fifty in ways that would have been impossible without the years of consistent presence. Time is the primary asset — and at thirty, there is an abundance of it.

The risk at thirty is impatience. The tendency to abandon the long game for the short one — to take the comfortable job that pays well and defer the building until later. Later keeps moving. The thirty-year-old who defers the build until their forties will have the same conversation with themselves ten years from now, only with a shorter runway.

At fifty, the long game is not shorter — it is more concentrated. The time horizon for traditional compounding is compressed. But the asset base is different. You have something the thirty-year-old cannot replicate: decades of accumulated experience, pattern recognition, professional relationships, and the credibility that comes from having done the work long enough to understand it at a level that cannot be faked.

The fifty-year-old who monetizes experience directly — through consulting, teaching, content, advisory work — is not competing with thirty-year-olds on the same terms. They are playing a different game entirely. One where depth beats speed. Where the client who needs the problem solved correctly the first time does not want the newest person in the field. They want the one who has seen twenty versions of this problem and knows exactly which solution holds.

The risk at fifty is writing off the time horizon as too short to build anything meaningful. It is not. A fifty-year-old who builds consistently for fifteen years — who develops the income streams, the audience, the owned assets, the consulting practice — arrives at sixty-five with something the traditional retirement path almost never produces: multiple sources of income that do not require full-time employment to sustain, and the skills to generate more of them if needed.

That is not a fantasy. It is the math of the long game applied to the timeline actually available.

— — —

What You Are Building For

There is a version of the long game that is purely financial. Accumulate enough. Reduce expenses enough. Reach the number. Stop.

That version is real and worth pursuing. But it is not the whole game.

The deeper version of the long game is about what you leave in the world that continues to matter after you are no longer actively maintaining it.

The book that finds the right person five years after you published it. The framework you taught a manager who now teaches it to their team. The consulting work that reorganized a small business and put ten people in a more stable situation. The content that answered a question someone had been carrying for months.

These are not monuments. They are ripples. Small, specific, human-scale contributions that continue to move through the world independently of your continued effort.

Building for the long game means building things with ripples — not just transactions that reset when they complete.

It means sending money to your kids not from a salary that required sixty percent of your life on the road, but from income streams you built and own. It means traveling with your wife because the work is done for the day and the day belongs to you — not because you accumulated enough vacation days to justify the trip.

It means arriving at the end of the productive years with the ability to say: I built something real. It exists independently of any company that ever employed me. It has my name on it. And it will keep finding people who need it long after I have moved on to whatever comes next.

That is the long game.

It starts today. With the next action.

Honest Reflections

> *What are you building — not earning, but building — that will still be generating value five years from now without requiring you to be physically present for every transaction? If the answer is nothing yet, what is the first step toward changing that?*
>
> *What does your retirement actually look like if you build the income streams available to you*

rather than depending on the ones the system provided? Run the honest numbers. What is the gap, and which lane closes it?

What is the legacy you are building in the smaller, real sense — the people whose work is better because of what you taught them, the content that will find the right person at the right moment, the money sent without calculating whether you can afford it? Name it specifically. It is already partially built.

What weight are you still carrying from what happened — the resentment, the replaying, the rehearsed arguments? What would it cost you to put it down? What would it free up if you did?

What does the day look like five years from now if the long game works? Not the income statement — the morning. The work. The trip. The people around you. Write it down. Then work backward from it to today.

Chapter 16: A Letter to the Spat-Out

To the person reading this in the first week –

I know where you are right now.

The shock is still fresh. The calendar that used to organize your entire existence has gone quiet. The phone that buzzed with meeting invites and action items is sitting there with nothing urgent on it, and somehow that silence is louder than the noise ever was.

You are running calculations in the back of your mind even when you are trying not to. How long can we sustain this. What the numbers actually look like. Whether the plan you had – the one built around a structure someone else controlled – is still a plan at all.

I want to tell you something directly.

You got this.

Not as a slogan. Not as the thing people say when they do not know what else to say. As a statement of fact grounded in everything you have just read. You do. We do.

You already know how to work hard. You did it for years inside a system that was never fully designed to reward you for it. You are about to find out what hard work feels like when it is pointed at something you actually own.

The difference is everything.

— — —

Early in my career, I was a year into my first part-time job. The manager of the cashiers — someone I respected, someone who had been a quiet influence on the way I thought about work — resigned unexpectedly.

I was sad to see her go. I went to my manager and told him so.

He listened. Then he said something I have carried for almost forty years.

"Remember — change is always the opportunity for positive change."

He was not minimizing the loss. He was reframing what it meant.

Every change — even the ones that arrive uninvited, even the ones that arrive in a ten-minute meeting with HR — contains the possibility of something better on the other side. Not automatically. Not without effort. But the possibility is real, and it belongs to you, and no one can take it away.

What happened to you was not fair. It may not have been right. But it opened a door.

You are standing in front of it right now.

— — —

Here is what I need you to know about what comes next.

It will be hard work at first. There is no version of this that skips the effort. You will have to learn things you did not expect to need to learn. Marketing. Platforms. How to find customers. How to put your work in front of people who do not already know your name. How to sustain output when the feedback loop is quiet and the traction has not yet arrived.

You will have days when the silence feels like failure. It is not. It is the gap between starting and momentum — and everyone who ever built anything real passed through it.

But here is the thing about the spiral.

Once it starts moving, it does not want to stop.

The first small win — a single sale, a comment from a stranger who found your work and felt something, a client who came back a second time — changes something. Not the math. The feeling. The confirmation that what you are building is real, that it is finding people, that you are not shouting into an empty room.

And from that first win, the next action is easier. And the one after that easier still. The confidence is not manufactured — it is earned, action by action, until one day you look back at the person who sat in the shock of the first week and barely recognize how far the distance has grown.

That spiral is waiting for you.

It starts with your first action. Take action.

— — —

I want to say something about the people around you.

If you have a partner who is steady — someone who looks at the situation clearly and says "we got this" without flinching — listen to them. They are seeing something you may not be able to see from inside the shock, from inside your panic. The person who can hold the long view when you are lost in the immediate is one of the most valuable things in a difficult season. Do not mistake their steadiness for not understanding. They understand. They are just not letting fear do the navigation.

And if you are reading this alone — without that steadiness beside you — then let this book be part of what holds the long view.

You are not the first person to stand here. You will not be the last.

And the ones who came through it — who built something real on the other side of the loss — did it by refusing to let the system's decision about their cost structure become the final word on their value.

You are not a cost.

You are a builder.

The system just reminded you of something you had forgotten.

— — —

A few things I want you to remember when the hard days come — and they will come.

The forty-hour week was not designed for your benefit. The retirement promise was a carrot that kept moving. The healthcare that felt like security was a tether. You know this now. Knowing it means you can build something that does not depend on any of it.

The legal answer, whatever it was, is the answer. That chapter is closed, but you may have some work to do with an attorney.

The energy you would spend on resentment is energy that belongs to the build.

Your skills belong to you. Every bit of expertise you developed — the pattern recognition, the problem-solving, the ability to walk into a broken situation and see exactly what needs to change — that traveled with you when they deactivated the badge.

The staff badge wasn't yours. It was the property of the company.

No company can take what you own. Your skills.

Position is built before you need it. You learned that lesson the hard way. Now you build it as a permanent practice so you never have to learn it again.

Action outweighs inaction. Every time. A flawed plan executed is worth more than a perfect plan contemplated. Start where you are. Use what you have. Learn and adjust as you go.

The day is coming.

The day when the work you are building right now — in the quiet of the early morning, in the hours that used to go to a commute, in the deliberate effort that no one is scheduling for you — starts to return something real.

A check that arrived because of something you built. A message from someone who found your work and needed it. A moment when you look at what you have created and understand that it belongs to you in a way that a salary never did.

That day is not guaranteed by reading this book. It is earned by what you do after you close it.

So here is what I want you to do.

Look at the notes you took. Read the Honest Reflections questions that landed hardest. Find the one that you have been avoiding because answering it honestly requires you to commit to something.

Answer it. Put it on paper and hang it on the wall above your desk.

Then clear off your desk.

Because you have work to do.

Not their work. Your work.

The work that builds the life you have been describing since Chapter 9 — two to three hours of focused creation, money rolling in from things you built and own, time with the people you love, the world open in front of you rather than visible only through an airport window on the way to someone else's quarterly review.

That life is not on the other side of the next job offer.

It is on the other side of the next action.

I took action and wrote this book for us.

You are ready.

Go build it for you.

You got this.

— MJ Carver

Afterword: Where to Go From Here

You made it to the end of this book.

And, so did I.

Which means you are ready to begin.

The notes you took — the Honest Reflections questions you sat with, the lanes you circled, the numbers you finally wrote down — those are the beginning of the plan. Not a finished plan. The beginning of one. And a beginning is enough to start moving.

— — —

I wrote this book because I needed it and it did not exist. Because when I walked out of that room and called my wife, I did not need a book that softened what had happened or reframed it into an opportunity. I needed one that told the truth about the system, stabilized the immediate panic, and then pointed clearly toward what to build instead.

I hope it was that book for you. It was for me.

If it was — if something in these pages landed at the right moment, or answered a question you had been carrying, or gave you the framework for a decision you needed to make — I would genuinely like to know. Not for the algorithm. Because that kind of feedback is what sustains the work between the writing of one book and the next.

Email me: mjmj2222@gmail.com

— — —

If you found value here, the single most useful thing you can do is leave an honest review wherever you purchased this book. Reviews are how books find the people who need them. And the person in their first week after a layoff, searching for something that tells the truth — they need to be able to find this.

If you are interested in consulting, coaching, or working through The Leverage Code framework with direct support, reach out. I built a career helping organizations and the people inside them work better. That work did not end when the badge was deactivated. It just moved to a context I actually own.

Email me: mjmj2222@gmail.com

Thank you for joining me on this journey through this book. It has helped me. I truly hope it has helped you.

Now it's your turn.

Go clear your desk.

You have work to do.

Go build your new life.

— MJ Carver

Acknowledgments

This book exists because of my wife.

Not in the way authors say that as a formality. In the literal sense that on the day the job ended, she was the one who said "we got this" — and meant it clearly enough that I believed it. She has been the voice of reason through every hard chapter of this story, including the chapters that did not make it into the book. She did not flinch when the income stopped. She did not pretend the difficulty was smaller than it was. And she was honest with me when honesty was harder to hear than reassurance would have been.

That kind of partnership is not common. I do not take it for granted.

— — —

I also want to acknowledge the managers I have worked with and alongside over the years — the ones who were voices of reason in difficult rooms, who were not afraid to say the hard thing, and who modeled what it looks like to lead without pretending. The ones who said "we got this" before the situation was resolved, not after. The ones who were honest even when the truth stung.

Good managers are rarer than they should be. The ones I have been fortunate enough to work with shaped how I think about leadership, accountability, and what it means to actually show up for the people in your care. This book is partly the result of watching them work.

— — —

And to the reader who picked this up in the first week after their layoff – or the tenth week, or the year after, still rebuilding – thank you for trusting this book with that moment. I wrote it for you. I hope it helped.

About the Author

MJ Carver spent decades inside corporate organizations as a process auditor and improvement director — the person leadership called when something was broken and needed to be rebuilt correctly. He has traveled extensively, coached managers, redesigned operations, and watched from the inside as the machine that employed him demonstrated, in a ten-minute meeting, exactly what it was designed to do.

He writes about responsibility, leadership, and the practical architecture of a life built on leverage and position rather than dependency and hope. His first book, The Leverage Code, laid the foundation for the framework that made it possible to absorb a layoff without panic and pivot toward something he actually owns. Love, Positioned, his second book, explores what it means to build a committed relationship with the same deliberateness most people reserve for their careers.

SPAT-OUT is his 2nd book — and the most personal. It was written from inside the experience, not from the comfortable distance of having already built and sorted. The traction is still building for him. The work is still in progress. He is not standing at the finish line telling you the view is worth it.

He is at his desk, building beside you.

— — —

MJ Carver's books are NOT available on Amazon.

He can be reached at mjmj2222@gmail.com – This email address was free, easy to remember, because not everything needs to be complicated.

If you want further information, and to sign up for his mailing list, please jump over to his website at: www.mjcarverbooks.com

If this book helped you, he would genuinely like to know.

A Note on Reviews

If this book found you at the right moment — if something in these pages helped you think more clearly, feel less alone, or take the next action — the most useful thing you can do is leave an honest review on any book site you have used to purchase my book.

Reviews are how books find the people who need them. The person in their first week after a layoff, searching for something that tells the truth, will find this book because someone like you said it was worth reading.

That is the whole ask. Thank you.

www.ingramcontent.com/pod-product-compliance
Lightning Source LLC
LaVergne TN
LVHW012044160826
845678LV00014B/2694

* 9 7 9 8 9 9 5 4 2 4 5 0 5 *